The New Contented Little Baby Book

The New Contented Little Baby Book

The secret to calm and confident parenting from one of the world's top maternity nurses

Gina Ford

Vermilion
LONDON

Dedication

To my beloved mother and best friend
in blessed remembrance of all her wisdom,
the very special love, support and encouragement
she always gave me and whose wonderful smile and
sparkling eyes could turn a rainy day into sunshine.

13 15 17 19 20 18 16 14 12

Text copyright © Gina Ford 1999, 2002

The right of Gina Ford to be identified as the author of this book has been asserted
by her in accordance with the Copyright, Designs and Patents Act 1988.

First published in the United Kingdom in 1999 by Vermilion
This edition published in 2002 by Vermilion
an imprint of Ebury Press
Random House
20 Vauxhall Bridge Road
London SW1V 2SA

Random House Australia (Pty) Limited
20 Alfred Street, Milsons Point, Sydney,
New South Wales 2061, Australia

Random House New Zealand Limited
18 Poland Road, Glenfield,
Auckland 10, New Zealand

Random House South Africa (Pty) Limited
Endulini, 5A Jubilee Road,
Parktown 2193, South Africa

Random House UK Limited Reg. No. 954009

A CIP catalogue record for this book is available from the British Library

ISBN: 0 09 188233 8

Printed and bound in Great Britain by
Mackays of Chatham Ltd, Chatham, Kent

Please note that conversions to imperial weights and measures are suitable equivalents
and not exact.

The information given in this book should not be treated as a substitute for qualified
medical advice; always consult a medical practitioner. Neither the author nor the
publisher can be held responsible for any loss or claim arising out of the use, or misuse,
of the suggestions made or the failure to take medical advice.

Contents

8   Introducing solid food   189

Acknowledgements

I would like to thank the Hodgsons for their wonderful friendship and constant support: Keith, for his invaluable help in transforming my Routines and Feeding Plans into at-a-glance form, so making easier reading for parents; and Janetta, for her endless patience and the late nights she spent helping transform my often very rough drafts into an understandable and readable manuscript for my editor Joanna Carreras. I thank Joanna for being so supportive and patient during the writing of this book and for all her excellent editorial changes and ideas.

A special debt of thanks to my dear cousin Sheila Eskdale and special friends Jane Revell and Joanne Amps. Their endless phone calls and notes of encouragement have given me enormous emotional support.

Finally, I would like to thank the hundreds of parents all over the world who have shared their babies with me. Without their experiences and continual feedback over the years this book would not have been possible.

Gina Ford

Foreword

The baby book that is different

With the massive amount of information and knowledge available on raising children from birth, it is a difficult task for new parents to know where to start. If you do have some spare time after pregnancy to read about postnatal care, you will find there is no information on how to cope day by day, and nothing to help you understand the changes that will occur on a week-to-week basis in a quick and easily digestible form.

This is where Gina comes to the rescue with her hour-by-hour, week-by-week guide on how to get a baby into a sensible routine. A series of clear guides chart the changes in the needs of baby and parents, so that at a glance you can see how to cope with this new way of life, one day at a time, from week to week.

Whether you are breast feeding or bottle feeding, Gina takes you through a typical day, helping you manage both the baby and your time, and teaches you to understand the changes that the baby will go through. Then as the feeding needs of your baby change, she demonstrates how to start the weaning process of introducing solids, with forward-looking advice on how and why to adapt the baby's menu.

All the 300 or so babies that Gina has helped look after are a happy testament to how a routine can help. Gina uses her hands-on experience on how to get the best for your baby and uses actual examples of problems she has encountered to help the reader to understand and solve the problems they might have.

Keith Hodgson

Father of Jake Jupiter Hodgson – born 2.1.96 – a true Gina baby, who sleeps 12 hours every night, has always eaten well and is happy and content in all ways.

Introduction

Most of the books about small babies on the market at present are written by doctors, psycholgists or people of that status. Their information is based on their own children, or parents and children who have participated in research studies. While the medical information and developmental text can be interesting, one would have to query how much help it can be to the average first-time mother getting to grips with the never-ending demands of a new baby.

For instance, most of the books will inform you that it is normal for a baby to wake up several times a night, and that you should feed on demand as often and for as long as your baby wants, and allow the baby to find his own sleep pattern. For the authors of these books this approach does not necessarily present a problem, as their work can probably be done at any time of the day to fit in with the baby sleeping. But what about the parents who have to get up at 7am to deal with older children or start a day's work around 9am? After a few weeks, these continual wakings can reduce even the sanest of human beings to complete wrecks. You will be told that things will get better, yet recent surveys show that 85 per cent of children are still waking up at night by the age of one year. The baby experts have no answer; many of them experience the same sleepless nights' syndrome themselves, but they probably do not suffer as much as other parents who are dictated to by a strict schedule and heavy work-loads.

Baby business is big business. Look at the shelves of any good bookshop; you will find literally dozens and dozens of baby books. Flick through the pages dealing with sleep and feeding and you will find the advice is nearly always the same: 'Rock your baby, walk the floor, nurse him to sleep on the breast, put him in a sling or drive him around the block in the car.' Every day thousands of parents are doing all of these things, some for months, others for years. They then go on to the second stage of reading: 'How to solve your children's sleep problems.' In these books you are told that the reason your baby has a sleep problem is that he has learned the wrong associations, ie rocking, feeding to induce sleep, driving around the block to induce sleep.

What is so different about my book is that it comes from years of hands-on experience. I have lived with and cared for hundreds of different babies. I offer real and practical advice on how to establish a good feeding and sleeping pattern from day one, thus avoiding months of sleepless nights, colic, feeding difficulties, and many of the other problems that the experts convince us are a normal part of parenting.

The routines will teach you to recognise the difference between hunger and tiredness and how to meet all your baby's needs, which will result in a very happy, contented baby, who is likely to sleep through the night at around six to ten weeks. My advice will teach you how to listen to what your baby is really saying. It has worked for hundreds of mothers and their babies all over the world; it can work for you too.

Finally, for no particular reason, and I hope this does not cause offence, the baby is always 'he'.

Preparation for the birth | 1

When one talks of preparing for the birth, the first things that spring to mind are antenatal care and decorating the nursery. Both are important in their own ways. Antenatal care is of the utmost importance for a healthy pregnancy and essential to prepare you for the birth, and decorating the nursery for the new arrival is fun. While many of the classes do give some advice on what is ahead after the birth, they often overlook very practical tips, which if offered early enough, could save the parents hours of time and stress after the baby is born.

If you follow my routines from day one you should be fortunate enough to have a content and happy baby with some time for yourself. However, as you will see from my routines and charts, spare time is extremely limited (and, believe me, mothers who are not following a routine have even less spare time). In this short amount of time, unless you have hired help, you will have to fit in the cooking of meals, shopping, laundry etc.

By doing the following things before the baby is born you will gain many hours of free time after the birth:

- Order all your nursery equipment well in advance. Cots can sometimes take up to 12 weeks to be delivered and there are many advantages in having the big cot from the beginning. (See page 3.)
- Have all the bed-linen, muslins and towels washed and ready for use. Make up the cot, Moses basket and pram. Prepare everything in the nursery so it is at hand the minute you get home from the hospital.

- Have all the baby essentials in stock: cotton wool, baby oil, nappies, nappy and moisturizing creams, baby wipes, soft sponges, baby brush, bath oil and baby shampoo.
- Check that all the electrical equipment is working properly. Learn how the sterilizer works and how to put together the feeding bottles.
- Arrange a section of work-top in the kitchen where preparation and sterilizing can be done. Ideally it should be directly below a cupboard where all the baby's feeding equipment can be stored.
- Stock up on soap powder, cleaning materials and enough kitchen and toilet rolls to last at least six weeks.
- Prepare and freeze a large selection of healthy home-made meals. If you are breast feeding you should avoid the shop bought ones that are full of additives and preservatives.
- Stock up on extra dry goods such as tea, coffee, biscuits etc; it is inevitable that you will have extra visitors the first month, and supplies will soon go down.
- Purchase gifts and cards for any forthcoming birthdays. Also have a good selection of thank-you cards ready to send for all the gifts you will receive.
- Get up to date with any odd jobs that need to be done in the house or garden. The last thing you need once the baby has arrived is the hassle of workmen to-ing and fro-ing.
- If breast feeding, book your electric expressing machine well in advance; they are in big demand!

The nursery

Like most parents, you will probably want to have your baby sleeping in your room with you during the night. However, never sleep with the baby in your bed: it's all too easy to roll over and cause suffocation. I can't stress enough though, the importance of having the nursery ready on your return from the hospital. All too often a mother will ring me up in a complete panic asking for advice on how to get a three-month-old baby used to their own room. Many tears and much anxiety could have been avoided if the mother had got the baby used to his own room from day one. Instead, for the first few weeks the baby dozes on and off during the early part of the evening in a car seat, then is taken to the parents' room for the last feed and the night. It is not surprising that these babies feel very abandoned when they are eventually put to sleep by themselves, in an unfamiliar dark room.

From the very beginning you should use the nursery for nappy changing and naps. In the evening after the bath, feed and settle the baby there from 7pm to 10pm. The baby can still be transferred to your room after the last feed, to make middle-of-the-night feeding easier. But by getting your baby used to his room from the beginning, he will very quickly enjoy being there and see it as a peaceful haven, not a prison.

When my babies are very small, if they have become over-tired or overstimulated, I find that they will calm down immediately when taken to their room. And by six weeks they are positively beaming when taken to their nursery for the bath and bedtime routine.

Decoration and furnishings

It is not essential to spend a fortune on decorating and furnishing the baby's room. A room with walls, windows and bed-linen covered in teddy bears soon becomes very boring. Plain walls can easily be brightened up with a colourful frieze, and perhaps a matching pelmet and tie-backs; this makes it easy to adapt the room as the baby grows, but avoids the need to redecorate totally. (Another very cost-effective and fun way to liven up the room is to use sheets of children's wrapping paper as posters, which are bright and colourful – and can be changed frequently.)

The following guidelines should be observed when choosing furnishings and fittings for the nursery.

The cot

Most baby books advise that in the early days a cot is not necessary, as babies are happier in a Moses basket or small crib. I am not convinced they are happier and sleep better in these. As I have mentioned earlier, I much prefer to get my babies used to their big cot from day one. By doing this I have never encountered a problem when they outgrow the Moses basket and start to sleep the whole night in their big cot in the nursery.

When choosing a cot it is important to remember that it will be your baby's bed for at least two or three years and it should be sturdy enough to withstand a bouncing toddler. Even very young babies will eventually move around their cot.

Choose a design with flat spars instead of round ones, as pressing his head against a round spar could be quite painful for a young baby. Cot bumpers are not advised for babies under one year old, as they often end up sleeping with their heads pressed up against the bumpers. Because body heat escapes through the top of the head, blocking this off causes the risk of overheating, which is thought to be a contributing factor in cot death.

The other points to look for when choosing a cot are:

- Choose one with two or three different base height levels.
- Drop-sides should be easy to put up and down without making a noise. Test several times.
- It should be large enough to accommodate a two-year-old child comfortably.
- All cots must comply with the recommendations set out by the British Standards Institute, Number BS1753. Spars must be no less than 2.5cm (1in) apart and no more than 6cm (2$1/2$in). When the mattress is in its lowest position, the maximum distance between that and the cot top should be no more than 65cm (26in). There should be a gap of no more than 4cm (1$1/2$in) around the edge of the mattress.
- Buy the best possible mattress that you can afford. I have found that foam mattresses tend to sink in the middle within a few months. The one that I have found to give the best support for growing babies is a 'natural cotton spring interior' type. All mattresses must comply with Safety Standards Numbers BS1877 and BS7177.

Bedding required for the cot

Everything should be 100 per cent white cotton so that it can be washed on a hot wash along with the baby's night clothes. Due to the risk of overheating or smothering, quilts and duvets are not recommended for babies under one year old. If you want a pretty matching top cover for your baby's cot, make sure it is 100 per cent cotton and not quilted with a nylon filling. For parents who are handy with a sewing machine, a considerable amount of money can be saved by making flat sheets and draw sheets out of a large cotton double-bed sheet.

Making up the cot

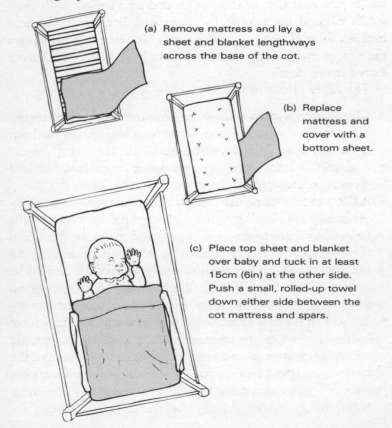

(a) Remove mattress and lay a sheet and blanket lengthways across the base of the cot.

(b) Replace mattress and cover with a bottom sheet.

(c) Place top sheet and blanket over baby and tuck in at least 15cm (6in) at the other side. Push a small, rolled-up towel down either side between the cot mattress and spars.

You will need a minimum of the following bedding:

- Three stretch cotton fitted bottom sheets. Choose the soft jersey-type cotton rather than the towelling type, which very quickly can become rough and worn looking.
- Three flat, smooth cotton top sheets. Avoid flannelette, which gives off too much fluff for young babies; this can obstruct the nose and cause breathing problems.
- Three cotton, small-weave cellular blankets, plus one wool blanket for very cold nights.
- Six flat, smooth cotton pram sheets. These are small sheets that are used for prams and small cribs, but are also ideal as draw sheets, which you put across the head end of the bottom sheet. This eliminates the need to remake the whole cot in the middle of the night, should your baby leak or dribble.

Changing station

There are special units designed as changing stations which have the changing mat placed on the top and two shelves below for nappies and all the other equipment needed. Again, like so much of the other specially designed baby equipment, they are not really practical. The main reasons are that the top is never large enough to include a top-and-tail washing bowl, so a further table is required at the side. It is also difficult to access items stored at the back of the shelves below, which are difficult to keep neat and tidy due to their depth.

By far the best type of changing station I have used is a long unit consisting of drawers and a cupboard. The top is long enough to hold the changing mat, and still leaves enough room at the bottom end to place the top-and-tail bowl and all the other things needed for nappy changing. The drawers can be used to store nightwear, underwear, bibs and muslins and the cupboard will hold larger items like packets of nappies and the top-and-tail bowl. Sometimes these units have a side extension table, which can be folded down when not in use, thus saving space.

If you are determined to have everything co-ordinated, I believe some nursery furniture manufacturers have a design like the long unit just described that matches their cot, but they are very expensive. By spending a little time searching it is possible to get something cheaper in a similar style, with a finish to match the cot.

Wardrobe

A fitted wardrobe is a very good investment for a nursery as it enables you to keep the baby's clothes neat, tidy and crease free and provides you with valuable storage space for the many other pieces of equipment that you will eventually accumulate. If possible, the fitted wardrobe is best built on a partition or a hall wall, as it will then have the advantage of helping to sound-proof the nursery.

If a fitted wardrobe is out of the question, try to purchase a free-standing one. These can often be picked up at the sales very cheaply. Do not be tempted to buy one of the 'cute' wardrobes designed especially for babies; I have found that within a few months they prove to be too small and totally impractical to meet the needs of fast-growing babies.

Chair

It is essential, no matter how small your baby's room is, that you try to fit in a chair. The ideal chair could also be used as a breast-feeding chair, so it should have a straight back, be wide enough to allow room for both you and your baby as he grows and have arms to support you while breast feeding. Later on it will support you as you hold your toddler while reading the bedtime story. Many parents are attracted to a rocking chair, but these can prove to be quite dangerous as your baby becomes more mobile and attempts to pull himself up holding on to the chair. In the early days it can also be tempting to settle the baby by rocking him to sleep, but this is one of the main causes of a baby developing poor sleeping habits.

Curtains

Curtains should be full length and fully lined with black-out lining. It is of the utmost importance that they are fixed to a track that fits flush along the top of the window. Ideally they should have a deep matching pelmet, which is also lined with black-out lining. There should be no gaps between the sides of the curtains and the window frame; even the smallest chink of light can be enough to wake your baby earlier than 7am. For the same reason, curtain poles should be avoided as the light streams out of the gap at the top. As the baby gets older he may not settle back to sleep if woken at 5am by early morning sun or street lights.

I am so convinced that a dark room encourages good sleeping habits that I will not take a booking unless the nursery has both curtains with black-out lining and a special black-out roller blind (see Useful Addresses). When the lights are off and the curtains closed, it should be so dark that you are unable to see your partner standing at the other side of the room. Research has also proved that the chemicals in the brain alter in the dark, conditioning it for sleep. This is one of the reasons why, in the early days, I put my babies in a dark room for all their naps.

Alexander: aged three years

Alexander was three years old when I went to care for his new-born sister. As a baby he was fed on demand, and on the advice of the maternity nurse was left to find his own sleep pattern. By nine months of age Alexander was still waking up several times a night and his parents were so exhausted and desperate for sleep that they decided to try the Richard Ferber sleep training method (see Further Reading). Over a period of one week, when he woke up in the night he was left to settle himself back to sleep; his parents would check him, but not talk to him. They gradually extended the checking time until they were not going in at all. By the end of the week he was sleeping through from 7pm to 5am, but once awake he was ready to begin the day. The parents accepted this early start to the day; after nine months of being woken several times a night they were just grateful that he actually slept a solid ten hours.

However, when they had their second baby they realized that Alexander's very early start and caring for a new-born baby would be very difficult. I suggested that they try putting him to bed later to see if he would sleep later, but they had tried this on many occasions and he would still wake at 5am.

They had also tried leaving him to cry, but this was quite difficult as he nearly always woke up yelling, 'I've done a poo'. If left for any length of time he would attempt to change his own nappy, which turned out to be a very messy business!

I observed Alexander for several days. Because of his early start he was exhausted by 11am and needed to go down for a nap; sometimes this nap would last two hours. I suggested they cut the nap back to a strict 45 minutes, as if left longer than this he would go back into a deep sleep and be very difficult to wake. I was also concerned about his diet, as obviously something was triggering his bowels to work very early in the morning. I advised that he should be given his main protein meal at lunch time, and stick to a carbohydrate tea. I was also concerned about the amount of fruit and dried fruit he consumed in the day, especially in the afternoon, so we made sure that he had most of his daily intake of fruit and dried fruit before 3pm. The change in diet certainly worked regarding his bowel movements, as he stopped doing a poo at 5am, but unfortunately he kept waking up.

I then realized that every time we went in to him at 5am he was standing at the window, which had no curtains and only a roller blind fitted. Although it was a black-out blind, as with all of this type of blind, the light shone out from the top and down the sides. I was convinced that this was the main reason he would not settle himself back to sleep. It was harder to convince his parents. However, the bedroom his baby sister occupied was fitted with a black-out blind and black-out lined curtains and at one month she slept through the night from her last feed and had to be woken at 7am every morning. This helped persuade Alexander's parents of the importance of a totally dark room, and we fitted the window with full-length curtains and a deep box pelmet, both lined with black-out fabric.

Now when Alexander woke up it was so dark he could no longer see his way to the window. I would go straight to him when he cried out and repeat the same words, no matter how many times I had to go in to him. I would say 'It's not morning yet; be a good boy and go back to sleep, until Daddy comes for you.' I would not get into a conversation with him; whatever he said I would just repeat the same words. Within one week he was still waking up at 5am, but very quickly going back to sleep until 7am. By the end of two weeks he was going from 7pm to 7.30am every night. A year later he continues to sleep until 7–7.30am and I am convinced that the main problem here was light. All babies and young children will come into a light sleep or wake between 5am and 6am, but if a room is dark enough, they will be much more likely to go back to sleep.

Alexander's sister, now aged 15 months, despite two colds and several trips abroad, has never woken up before 7am. When the family travels, the first thing that is packed is two lengths of attachable black-out linings!

Carpeting

A fully fitted carpet is preferable to rugs, which can be a potential danger for tripping on when you are attending to your baby in the dim light. Choose a carpet that is treated with a stain-guard and avoid very dark or bright colours as they tend to show the dirt more easily.

Lighting

If the main light is not already fitted with a dimmer switch, it would be worthwhile to change it. In the early days, dimming the lights when settling the baby is a good association signal. If you are on a limited budget, purchase one of the small plug-in night lights that fit into any normal 13amp electrical socket. I always use one of these lights in the middle of the night, regardlesss of whether a dimmer switch is fitted.

Baby equipment

Moses basket or small crib

As I mentioned earlier, a Moses basket is not really essential. Even the cheapest of Moses baskets and a stand can cost over £50, which is quite a lot of money for something inessential that your baby will outgrow within six weeks. However, if you live in a very large house or plan to travel in the first few weeks, it may be useful. If your budget is limited, try to borrow one from a friend and buy a new mattress.

A crib is a smaller version of a big cot. Certainly it is much longer than a Moses basket, but not really any more practical. Because we now put our babies to sleep on their backs, these narrow cribs create a problem for small babies. They wake themselves up several times a night because the cribs are not wide enough for them to sleep with their arms stretched out fully, and they get their hands caught between the spars.

If you do decide to use either of the above for a short period you will need the following bedding:

- Three fitted, stretch cotton bottom sheets. Choose the soft, smooth jersey-type cotton.
- Six smooth cotton flat pram sheets, to be used as top sheets and later as draw sheets on the big cot.
- Four cotton, cellular close-weave pram blankets.
- A dozen muslins to be placed across the top of the basket or crib to catch dribbles.

Pram

The traditional pram is very expensive and not really appropriate to modern-day living. Most parents find it more practical to choose one of the other smaller types of transport available now. When choosing a pram, carry-cot or buggy, it is important to take into consideration where you live and your lifestyle. For example, if you have to drive to the nearest shops, it is important to choose a buggy that is easy to put up and down and not too heavy for constant lifting in and out of the car boot. There are now some very lightweight buggies on the market that recline flat for a newborn baby, and come with hood and apron to give the baby some protection in cold weather.

Another popular choice with parents is a 'three-in-one', which is a transporter that can be used with a carry-cot in the early days and later with a buggy type seat. This can be a very good choice if you live in a quieter area and can walk to the local shops. The third choice is a heavier-weight version of the light buggy; it also reclines flat for a newborn and usually comes with a mattress.

If you are likely to be using your pram or buggy in a town area, or in shops with narrow spaces (eg aisles in supermarkets) swivel wheels are a godsend. They make turning the buggy or pram round corners effortless compared to those with set wheels.

Whatever type you choose, you should practise putting it up and down several times, and try lifting it on to a surface in the shop to get an idea of how easy it is going to be to lift into the boot.

The following guidelines should also be observed when purchasing a pram, carry-cot or buggy:

- It should be fitted with good strong safety straps that go over the baby's shoulders as well as around the waist, and have an easy-to-operate brake. Make sure it has a hood and apron to protect the baby in colder weather.
- Buy all the extras at the same time: sun canopy, rain cover, cosytoes cover, head support cushion and shopping tray or bag. Models often change in design and sometimes dimension, and if you wait till the following season, the items you require might not fit or match.
- Try pushing it around the shop to check if the handle height is a comfortable level; also observe how easy it is to get in and out of doorways and round corners.

Car seat

A car seat should always be used, even for the shortest of journeys. Never be tempted to travel holding your baby in your arms. If the car had to stop suddenly or, even worse, was in a collision, tests have proved that it is impossible to keep hold of the baby. It is also dangerous to put the baby's car seat on the front seat of a car fitted with air bags. Some seats come with adjustable backs and a rocking mode so that they can double up as a seat in the house. As with the cot, choose the best you can afford and one that comes with very clear instructions on how to fit the seat. Things to look for when choosing a car seat are:

- A seat with large side wings that will give your baby more head protection from a side-on impact collision.
- A car seat fitted with a one-pull harness will make it much easier to adjust to suit the needs of your baby's clothing.
- The buckle should be easy to open and close, but not easy enough for a child to open.
- Look for extra accessories like a sun shade, head support pillow and replacement cover.

Baby bath

A baby bath is another item that is not essential. Like the Moses basket, babies outgrow the small bath very quickly. A newborn baby can be bathed in the hand basin to begin with, or even a big bath using one of the several types of bath seats that are available for tiny babies. These allow the baby to lie, supported and on a slight slope, leaving the mother with both hands free to wash the baby.

If you would feel more confident with a special baby bath, the one I would recommend is designed to fit across a big bath. It makes filling and emptying much easier, unlike the traditional baby bath that sits on a stand, and has to be filled and emptied using a bucket. Another design is a bath that is incorporated in a changing station. I have found these totally impractical because as you lift the baby out of the bath you have to manoeuvre the lid, which doubles as the changing table, down over the top of the bath before you can put the baby on it to dry and dress him. They are also very difficult to empty; I found I always had to tip the whole thing on its side to drain the water out completely. This usually ended up with all the items stored below toppling out on to the floor. These bath/changing stations are very expensive and I would discourage anyone from buying them.

Changing mat

It is worthwhile buying two changing mats and keeping the spare one downstairs. Choose them in plastic for easy cleaning, with well-padded sides. In the early days it is best to lay a hand towel on the top, as very young babies hate to be laid down on anything cold.

Baby monitor

This is another piece of equipment on which I would not advise skimping. There are two types to choose from: plug-in and mobile, and I always advise parents to go for the mobile one. They usually have a clip that can be attached to a pocket or belt, allowing you to move freely around the house. This is very useful if you want to take a bath or nip to the garage, places that often do not have an electrical power point. Most have a sound-activated visual light display that allows you to turn the volume down but still monitor whether the baby is crying or not. The one with the best sound quality, and the most portable that I have used, is a rechargeable one, which has a very small portable unit within the parent unit. It is the most expensive on the market, but well worth the extra money.

When choosing a baby monitor look for the following:

- Monitors work using radio frequencies so choose a model with two channels, allowing you to switch channels if there is interference.
- A rechargeable model is more expensive initially, but the saving on batteries will make it cheaper in the long run.
- A low-battery indicator and an out-of-range indicator.

Baby sling

Some parents swear by this method of moving around with their babies. I never use one as I find it too big a strain on my back to carry a baby around like this for any length of time.

Very small babies are also inclined to go straight to sleep the minute you hold them close to your chest, which defeats the whole purpose of my routines, ie keeping the baby awake at certain times of the day, and teaching the baby the right associations of going to sleep on his own. I do think that as babies get bigger slings are a very useful way for parents to carry them around, especially when the baby is old enough to face forward.

If you feel a sling would be useful, the following guidelines should be observed when choosing one:

- It should have safety tabs to ensure that it cannot come undone.
- It must provide your baby with enough head and neck support; some come with a detachable cushion that gives extra support for very young babies.
- It should offer the choice of the baby facing in or outwards, and have a seat with an adjustable height position.
- It should be made of a strong washable fabric, with comfortable padded shoulder straps.

Baby chair

While many parents use the car seat in the house for the baby to sit in during the day, if your budget will stretch to it, a second seat for the home can be great bonus as it saves having to move the same seat from car to house.

A baby seat is designed differently from a car seat; the rigid type will have adjustable seat positions and a base that can either remain stable or be changed to a rocking mode. These chairs can also be used for your baby to sit in during the early stages of weaning.

Another type of seat available is called a 'bouncy chair'. This is a very lightweight seat made up of a steel frame covered in fabric and is designed to bounce as the baby moves. I have found them very popular with babies over two months, but they can be frightening to some tiny babies. Whatever type of chair you choose make sure your baby, no matter how tiny, is securely strapped in and never leave him unsupervised in either type of chair. Finally, always place your baby on the floor when he is in his seat; never be tempted to leave him on a table or work top.

Whichever type you decide to buy, observe the following guidelines:

- The frame and base should be firm and sturdy, and be fitted with a strong safety strap.
- Choose one with an easily removable and washable cover.
- Purchase a head support cushion for tiny babies.

Playpen

Nowadays playpens are often frowned upon, as some 'baby experts' feel they hinder the baby's natural instinct to explore. While no baby should be left for long periods in a playpen, they can be very useful for ensuring that your child is safe when you are preparing lunch or need to go to the bathroom or answer the door. If you decide to use a playpen, get your baby used to it from a very young age.

Some parents use their travel cot as a playpen, but if you have the space I recommend the square wooden type, which is much larger and enables the baby to pull himself up easily and to walk around. Whichever type you choose, make sure that it is situated out of reach of radiators, curtains, trailing flexes, etc; and never hang toys on pieces of string in the playpen as this could be fatal if your baby got tangled up in the string. Babies have been known to strangle themselves this way.

Important points to look for when choosing a playpen are:

- Make sure it has a fixed floor so that the baby cannot move it.
- Check that there are no sharp metal hinges or catches on which your baby can harm himself.

- If choosing a mesh-type playpen or travel cot, make sure that the mesh is strong enough to prevent your baby pushing small toys through and making a hole big enough to trap his hand or fingers.

Equipment needed for breast feeding

Nursing bra

These are bras made with specially designed cups that can either be unhooked or unzipped, making breast feeding easier. It is important that you choose a well-fitting bra with wide adjustable shoulder straps to help support your breasts. The bra should not press tightly against the nipples, as this can cause blocked milk ducts. As you will need to wear your bra day and night, you may find cotton ones preferable to polyester. Buy two before the birth, and once your milk has come in, if they prove to be comfortable a further two can be purchased.

Breast pads

In the early days you will use lots of breast pads as they will need to be changed every time your baby feeds and, if your breasts fill up quickly, sometimes in between feeds. Most of my mothers prefer the round ones, contoured to fit the breasts. The more expensive brands usually work out cheaper in the long run, as they are normally more absorbent. Buy one box at first and if that brand is suitable, you can then stock up with them.

Nursing pillow

These pillows are shaped to fit around a mother's waist, bringing small babies up to the perfect height for breast feeding. They can also be used for propping babies up, and make an excellent back support for older babies who are learning to sit up. Make sure you choose one with a removable, machine-washable cover.

Nipple creams and sprays

These creams and sprays are supposed to help care for the breasts and relieve them of any pain caused by breast feeding. As discussed in the breast-feeding section, poor positioning of the baby on the breast is usually the main cause of pain. If you experience pain when you are feeding your baby it would be wise to consult your health visitor or breast feeding counsellor before using a cream or spray. She will check that you are positioning the baby on the breast correctly, and advise on which cream or spray, if any, should be used. No other special creams or soaps are recommended when breast feeding. Wash your breasts twice a day with plain water and after each feed the nipples should be rubbed with a little breast milk and allowed to air dry.

Electric expressing machine

I am convinced that one of the reasons the majority of my mothers are so successful at breast feeding is because I encourage the use of an electric expressing machine. In the very early days when they are producing more milk than their baby needs (especially first thing in the morning) I get them to express from the second breast, using one of these very powerful expressing machines. The expressed milk is then stored in the fridge or freezer and can be used as a top-up later in the day when sometimes the mother's milk supply is low. This, I believe, is one of the main reasons why so many babies are restless and will not settle after their bath in the evening. The other advantage of expressing in the early days is when the baby goes through a growth spurt, the mother simply expresses less, immediately providing the baby with the extra milk he needs. This avoids her going back to demand feeding for several days in order to increase her milk supply, which is the usual advice given for increasing the milk supply during growth spurts.

If you want to breast feed and quickly establish your baby in a routine, an electric breast pump will be a big asset. Do not be persuaded to go for one of the smaller hand versions; they are much slower at drawing the milk off, which is one reason why so many women give up expressing. When ordering your breast pump it is worthwhile buying an additional expressing kit, which will save you having to sterilize the equipment immediately after use.

For information about where to hire a breast pump, see Useful Addresses at the end of this book.

Freezer bags

Expressed milk can be stored in the fridge for up to 24 hours, or in the freezer for one month. These specially designed pre-sterilized bags are an ideal way to store expressed breast milk and are available from most chemists and baby departments in the larger stores.

Feeding bottles

Most breast-feeding counsellors are totally against newborn babies being given a bottle, even of expressed milk. They claim that it creates nipple confusion and reduces the baby's desire to suck on the mother's breast, which leads to a poor milk supply and the mother giving up breast feeding altogether. My own view is that the majority of women give up breast feeding because they are totally exhausted by demand feeding, often several times a night. From the first week all my babies are introduced to a bottle of either expressed milk or formula milk; this one bottle a day is either given last thing in the evening or during the night. This allows my mothers to sleep for several hours at a stretch so they are much more able to cope with breast feeding. I have never had the problem of a baby rejecting the mother's breast, or becoming confused between the nipple and the teat. However, I do believe that this could happen if in the early days a baby was allowed more than one bottle a day.

A problem about which I receive a considerable number of

telephone calls is the one of older babies refusing a bottle. These babies have been breast fed exclusively, usually for three or four months. The mother is often returning to work, and finds that her baby absolutely refuses the bottle. This can lead to an enormous battle and weeks of struggling to get him to take a bottle – another good reason for getting your baby used to one bottle a day. Finally, it also gives the father a wonderful opportunity to become more involved.

There are many types of bottle available, with each manufacturer claiming it provides the 'best bottle' for your baby. Over the years I have tried and tested every available one, and the one that I have found to be the absolute best is the wide-necked design by AVENT. The wide neck makes cleaning and filling easier, and I support their claim that the design of the teat, being similar in shape to the mother's nipple, reduces the amount of wind a baby gets into his stomach. I suggest that you start off by using them with a slow-flow teat. This will make your baby work as hard drinking the milk from the bottle as he does when he is breast feeding.

For advice on the sterilizing equipment needed for your baby's feeding bottles, see page 22; for expressing advice refer to page 51.

Equipment needed for bottle feeding

Feeding bottles

For the reasons already discussed, I strongly advise mothers to pay a little extra money and purchase the wide-necked bottles described above. With babies who are taking all their milk from a bottle it is important that the risk of developing colic or wind is kept to the minimum. I have learnt from experience how babies being fed from cheaper bottles can develop wind. When called upon to help a baby with colic, I see an immediate improvement when I switch to feeding the baby with these wide-necked bottles. The designed teat is flexible and allows the baby to suckle as he does at the breast, but reduces the amount of air the baby takes in during a feed. By using these bottles, structuring the baby's feeds and following my routines, I have to date managed to solve all the colic problems with which I have been called upon to deal.

The wide-necked bottles also have the advantage that they can eventually be adapted to a feeding cup with soft spouts and handles. I would advise you to start off with five 240ml (8oz) bottles and three 120ml (4oz) bottles.

Teats

Most feeding bottles come with a slow-flow teat designed to meet the needs of newborns. By eight weeks I find that all my babies are feeding better from a medium-flow teat. It is worthwhile stocking up with these extra teats from the beginning.

Bottle brush

Proper and thorough cleaning of your baby's bottles is of the utmost importance. The best bottle brush comes with an extra-long plastic handle, which allows more force to be put into cleaning the bottles than with those that have either shorter plastic or wire handles.

Teat brushes

Most mothers find it easier to clean the teat by using their forefinger; however, if you have extra-long nails it may be worthwhile to invest in one of these brushes. The disadvantage with them is that it is all too easy to damage the hole of the teat, resulting in the need to replace the teats frequently. Of course, the same damage could be done with extra-long sharp nails!

Washing-up bowl

It is easier to organize and keep track of what is sterilized if all the dirty bottles are washed and sterilized at the same time. You will need somewhere to put the rinsed-out dirty bottles etc until they are ready to be sterilized. A large stainless steel or plastic bowl (ideally with a lid) can be used for this purpose; in addition it can be used for washing the bottles and any other equipment that needs to be sterilized.

Sterilizer

Whether breast or bottle feeding it is essential that all bottles and expressing equipment is sterilized properly. There are three main methods of sterilization: boiling all the equipment for ten minutes in a large pan, soaking in a sterilizing solution for two hours and rinsing with boiling water, or using a specially designed electric steam sterilizer. I have tried and tested all three methods many times and without doubt the easiest and fastest, and the one I believe to be the most efficient, is the steam sterilizer. It is well worth paying the extra money for the convenience these sterilizers provide. A word of warning. Do not be tempted to purchase the microwave version of these sterilizers. This particular unit not only holds fewer bottles, but it also becomes a complete nuisance when you have to keep removing it to use the microwave for cooking.

Electric bottle warmer

An electric bottle warmer is not really essential as formula can always be heated by standing the bottle in a jug of boiling water. However, an electric bottle warmer can be very useful in the nursery for the 6–6.30pm feed, as it saves having to take a jug of boiling water upstairs. There is a design that includes a bowl which fits on the top, and this can be used for keeping food warm once your baby starts on solids.

Bottle insulator

This is a special type of Thermos which is designed to keep bottles of boiled water warm. This can be very useful for travelling or for night feeds; it means that a feed can be prepared in seconds!

When buying a bottle insulator, it is advisable to purchase a small plastic three-section container; each section can hold the required scoops of milk powder for three different feeds. This avoids having to take the whole tin of formula milk powder on a day out, or upstairs for the middle-of-the-night feed.

Clothes for the newborn

The range of babywear now available in the shops is enormous, and eager sales assistants will be more than happy to advise you on a very long list of so-called essentials for your newborn baby. While it can be fun choosing a wide array of garments for your baby, I urge parents to approach with caution. Newborn babies grow at an alarming rate and will outgrow most of the first size clothes by the first month. Although it is important to have enough clothes to allow for the frequent changing of a newborn, it is foolish to end up having so many things hanging in the wardrobe that most of them never get worn. You will need to renew your baby's wardrobe at least three times in the first year, and even if you buy the cheapest of baby clothes it will still be a costly business.

I advise all parents to purchase only the basics until after the baby is born. When buying outfits for daywear remember that you will probably receive many of these as presents, so only buy the minimum. As I mentioned earlier, you will have considerable opportunity during the first year for clothes shopping.

When choosing clothes for the first month do not be tempted into buying brightly coloured underwear or nightwear. Believe me, it is impossible to keep these clean; newborn babies have a tendency to leak from both ends and the stains, despite what soap powder manufacturers say, are impossible to remove on anything less than a 60° wash. Brightly coloured garments soon lose their appearance if washed at a hot temperature, so leave the brighter colours for the outer garments.

Listed below are the basic items you will need for the first couple of months. I advise parents not to unwrap them until after the baby is born, so should you give birth to either a very large or very small baby they can be exchanged.

Vests	6–8	Socks	2–3 pairs
Nightdresses or sleepsuits	4–6	Hats	2
Day outfits	4–6	Mittens	2 pairs
Cardigans	2–3	Shawl	3
Snowsuit for a winter baby	1	Jacket	1

Vests

A newborn baby would normally wear a vest both winter and summer except in very hot weather. 100 per cent cotton is the best fabric next to a baby's skin, as polyester does not allow the baby's skin to breathe and wool brings some babies out in a rash. If you want to avoid your beautiful new layette becoming grubby looking or washed out by the very hot wash needed to remove stains, stick to plain white, or white with a pale colour pattern.

Without a doubt, the best style to buy is what is called a 'body suit'. It fastens under the baby's legs, has short sleeves and an envelope-type neckline, which enables you to either bring it over the baby's head easily, or to slip it on from the bottom. Avoid the traditional cross-over type of vests; they tend to ride up leaving the chest bare, and the ties constantly come undone.

Nightwear

In recent years it has become fashionable to put babies to sleep in baby-grows. While they may save a short amount of time on the laundry, they can cause hours of waking time in the night, as any experienced mother will tell you. You can spend 40 minutes feeding the baby and settling him, only to find he then fills his nappy. By the time you unpop all the fasteners, and struggle in the dim light to fasten them up again, even the most placid of babies is usually wide awake, possibly for another 40 minutes. As with vests, 100 per cent white cotton is best. The simpler the design, the better. Avoid anything with ties at the neck and if there are ties at the bottom, remove them, as they could become undone and get caught round the baby's feet.

Day outfits

During the first couple of months many mothers find it easier to buy baby-grows, which usually come in packs of two or three. They are made either of cotton or cotton and polyester. If possible, try to get 100 per cent cotton. However, if something with 80 per cent cotton and 20 per cent man-made fibre takes your eye, buy it and use it for when the baby is out and about in his pram or awake in his chair. Avoid putting him down to sleep all night in a garment that is not 100 per cent cotton as this could increase the risk of over-heating.

As these garments are worn only at night, they are less likely to get stained, so you can give them a quick wash by hand. Obviously it allows you a greater choice of colours when you do not have to worry about stains.

When choosing a garment, always try to find one that opens up either across the back or inside the legs, as it saves you having to undress the baby totally every time he needs a nappy change. Try to buy at least a couple of the dungaree-style clothes, without feet and with matching tee shirts. They last a bit longer than an all-in-one and the tops can be interchanged if the baby dribbles a lot. Choose ones in a soft velour-type fabric for very young babies.

Cardigans

If you have a summer baby you could probably get away with just two cardigans, ideally in cotton. With a winter baby it is best to have at least three cardigans. Although often hard to find, I firmly believe that wool is best for the winter. As long as the baby has a cotton garment next to his skin, there should be no cause for irritation and the simpler the design the better. While the very lacy patterned garments with ribbons are enchanting, be aware that little fingers can get entangled in these if they become undone, which could be dangerous. Perhaps two plain ones, and one fancier one for special occasions would be the answer.

Socks

Old-fashioned bootees and socks with fancy ribbons should be avoided, and should only be used for special occasions as they are dangerous for the same reasons as lacy cardigans: entangling little fingers and toes. Therefore simple socks, again in cotton or wool, are by far the most practical. It is probably worth mentioning here that no matter how cute they seem, shoes are not a good idea for small babies, as they could harm their soft bones.

Hats

In the summer it is important that you buy a cotton hat with a brim to protect your baby's head and face from the sun. Ideally the brim should go right round the hat to shade the back of the neck. In the spring and autumn it is possible to buy knitted cotton hats, which are more than adequate on cooler days. During the winter on very cold days, I would advise that a very fine wool bonnet is preferable. If the baby has a very sensitive skin, put a very thin cotton hat underneath it.

Mittens

I believe that small babies do not like their hands being covered up as they use them to touch, feel and explore everything with which they come in close contact. However, if your baby has very sharp nails you could try the plain fine cotton mitts made for this purpose. In very cold weather use simple wool mittens; again, put cotton ones underneath if your baby has a sensitive skin.

Shawl

I firmly believe that during the first few weeks all babies sleep better when swaddled. Whether you choose a blanket or a shawl to swaddle your baby, it should always be made of a very lightweight 100 per cent cotton fabric that has a slight stretch to it. When swaddling the baby it is important not to double the shawl. To avoid overheating always swaddle the baby in a single layer. Remember, when putting your baby to sleep swaddled, to reduce the number of blankets on the cot.

How to swaddle your baby

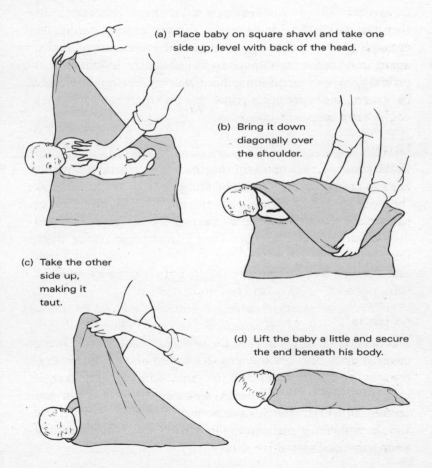

(a) Place baby on square shawl and take one side up, level with back of the head.

(b) Bring it down diagonally over the shoulder.

(c) Take the other side up, making it taut.

(d) Lift the baby a little and secure the end beneath his body.

However, it is very important that by the end of six weeks you start to get your baby used to being half swaddled (under the arms). Cot death rates peak between two and four months and over-heating is considered to play a major factor in cot death. Furthermore, only on the very coldest of nights would a blanket need to be added – always check that you are not putting too many layers on, and that the temperature of the room remains between 16–20°C (60–68°F), as recommended by the Foundation for the Study of Infant Deaths.

Snowsuit

When choosing a snowsuit for a winter baby always buy it at least two sizes too big as this allows plenty of room for growth. Avoid fancy designs with fur around the hood or dangling toggles, and choose one in an easy-care washable fabric. For very small babies one with poppers is preferable to one with a zip, which often digs into the baby's chin.

Jacket

A lightweight jacket can be useful for babies born at any time of the year. In the summer it can be worn on chilly days, and in the winter it can be worn on milder days. As with the snowsuit choose a simple design in a washable fabric, preferably with buttons, and again, two sizes too big.

Your baby's laundry

Having spent a considerable amount of time and money on your baby's wardrobe it is well worth the effort to be very fussy about caring for it. Because young babies grow out of their clothes so quickly it should be possible to pass them on to any brother or sister that follows. Sadly this often cannot be achieved as poor laundering means that a whole new layette is needed for the next baby.

The following guidelines will help keep your baby's clothes in tiptop condition:

- Laundry should be sorted into different coloured lots.
- Bedding, muslins and bibs need to be washed on a very hot wash to get rid of bacteria caused by milk stains and to eliminate the house dust mite, which can trigger off allergies in very young babies.
- Load the washing machine no more than two-thirds full so that the clothes are rinsed thoroughly.
- Stains should always be treated before washing.

Whites: 60°–90°

Anything that is stained should be soaked overnight in a cold solution of Napisan, then washed at 60°. Everything should be 100 per cent cotton, and bibs or towels with a coloured trim should have been tested for colour run by washing separately for the first few washes. Sheets, muslins, vests, bibs, socks and white sleepsuits and nighties can also go in at 60° if they are not very dirty. If they have not been soaked and are very dirty they should go in a 90° wash. Towels and face cloths should be washed and dried together, but separately from other clothes, to prevent their fluff sticking to other articles.

Light colours: 40°

Most day clothes need only a quick wash in the wool or delicate cycle. Anything stained should be soaked first overnight in cold water and Napisan and rinsed before washing.

Dark colours: 30° or hand wash

Any dark outfits must be washed separately from the light colours even if they do not run; to mix the two will only result in the lighter colours taking on a grey tinge. Anything stained should be soaked first overnight in cold water and baby soap powder.

Woollens or delicates: hand wash

Even if the label says 'machine wash' it is better to hand wash using a very small amount of Filetti (baby soap powder) mixed with lukewarm water. Always squeeze the garment gently in the water when washing and rinsing; never wring, twist or allow a saturated delicate garment to hang down. Rinse thoroughly in cool running water, gently squeeze out excess water, then roll in a clean, dry, white towel for a few hours. Finally, gently pull into shape and dry flat on a drying screen. Never hang up wet woollens.

Tumble drying

Towels, bibs, fitted cot sheets and blankets can be tumble dried, but flat cotton sheets and draw sheets should be dried so that they are slightly damp for easier and smoother ironing. Avoid drying towels and clothes together as it causes bobbling. Remove all clothes from the dryer and fold them as soon as possible to avoid creasing and ensure that all clothes are properly aired.

To avoid corduroy and dark clothes fading and shadowing, dry them on the cool cycle for no more than 15 minutes. Then pull the clothes into shape and hang them up on hangers to dry. In this way they may not need to be ironed.

Ironing

Flat cot sheets and draw sheets should be ironed slightly damp for a smooth finish. Light-coloured outfits should be ironed using the water spray and dark colours must be ironed on the inside with a very cool iron. Knitwear should be pressed under a damp a muslin cloth. Ensure that all labels are ironed flat.

After the birth

Leaving the hospital

During your stay in hospital you may be, like many of my mothers, counting the hours until you leave. However, when the actual day arrives, do not be surprised if you have feelings of fear and anxiety. This is very normal, especially for first-time mothers who are faced with the sudden realization that they are totally responsible for all the needs of this very precious tiny human being. Without the help and support of the nursing staff everything can suddenly seem very overwhelming. To eliminate these feelings as soon as possible, it is important that you plan your homecoming very carefully. It is essential that all family and friends are warned well in advance that you wish to keep the first week as calm and quiet as possible.

Obviously a new baby always brings much joy and excitement and you do not want to deny family and close friends the pleasure of sharing this. However, it is critical that your baby has time to adjust to his new surroundings. Some babies can be a little unsettled on leaving the hospital, and this can often be made much worse when they are subjected to endless handling, passed from one person to another. It is also essential that you allow time for you and your husband to get used to having this very special little person in your life, and even more importantly, time to learn how to meet his many very different needs. This is very difficult to achieve if you have a constant stream of visitors during the first week, and the phone never stops ringing.

The calmer and quieter things are, the sooner you will start to feel confident about caring for your baby. Do not feel guilty about delaying visits from friends for the first week or so. The prime consideration must be your baby, especially in the early days of breast feeding, as tiredness can seriously affect your milk production. Babies are also sensitive to their mother's emotions, and your baby will become very unsettled if he senses you are overtired and stressed.

If your husband is not able to take time off work for you and the baby's first week at home, try to arrange some sort of help. If your mother (or mother-in-law) will help, but not try to take over, and if she respects that you want to do things your own way, then see if she can come for a few days. If she lives near enough to pop in for a few hours each day, do not be afraid to request help with the cooking of meals, shopping or laundry. The more rest you can get in the first week at home the better.

Breast feeding: what to expect

Babies often become unsettled for the first few days at home. A well-meaning grandmother may try to convince you that your baby's fretfulness is due to hunger, that you are probably not producing enough milk to satisfy him or that your milk is of poor quality. These remarks, no matter how well-intentioned they are, can be very distressing for a new mother, who desperately wants breast feeding to be a success. Please be reassured that once your milk is in, if your baby totally empties a breast at every feed and is offered the other one, he will not go hungry. In my experience, formula-fed babies can be just as fretful the first few days at home, which discounts the 'hunger myth'.

Remember that your baby needs to feed little and often during the first week to help stimulate a good milk supply. Unless advised by the hospital, ignore any pressure to top him up with formula. This is old-fashioned advice and the fastest way to end up formula feeding. The exceptions to this rule would be if you had suffered a very bad delivery and were left feeling very weak, or if you had given birth to a very large baby. In these circumstances I would suggest that the baby be given one formula feed late at night, to allow the mother some much-needed rest.

If you follow my guidelines for establishing breast feeding in Chapter 3 (see page 38), along with my routines, you will find that you will very quickly build up a good milk supply and have a very contented and well-fed baby. I have mothers who, by following my advice, manage successfully to breast feed their second, third and fourth babies.

In the first few weeks if you express and freeze any extra milk you have in the early part of the day, you will ensure that when your baby goes through a growth spurt at three weeks, you will easily be able to meet his increased demands. It could also be used to top up your baby after the 6.15pm feed if he is not settling and you feel the reason could be that your milk is low.

Bottle feeding: what to expect

Within a few days most formula-fed babies have established some sort of feeding pattern, if they are drinking the required amount of formula at each feed for their weight. Do not be tempted to let your baby go longer than four hours between feeds during the day. To ensure that he only wakes for one feeding in the night, he needs to take the majority of his daily milk requirements between 7am and 11pm. A baby who is allowed to sleep five to six hours between feeds during the day would actually be two feeds short by 11pm. He would more than likely wake up two or three times in the night to try and satisfy his hunger. When this happens a mother is often so tired that she allows him to sleep well past the 7am feed in the morning, and a pattern emerges of the baby feeding more in the night than during the day.

During the first few weeks try to stick to the daily recommended amounts for your baby's weight, give or take a few ounces. Bottle-fed babies can become quite distracted when feeding, as they have more opportunity to look around, so try to keep feeding time calm and quiet. Do not overstimulate or talk to him too much, as this can cause him to lose interest in the feed. Be guided by your baby as to when he is ready to be burped; if the wind does not come up within a few minutes, leave it and try later. Keep referring to the sections on establishing bottle feeding and structuring milk feeds in Chapter 3, to make sure you increase the right feeds at the correct times.

Bonding: what to expect

The amount of attention and focus currently given by the media to 'a mother's love' and 'bonding' gives the impression that the majority of mothers do not know how to love their babies. Hardly a day passes by without a magazine or newspaper featuring a double-page spread of some celebrity mother, looking absolutely radiant as she cradles her designer-clad newborn baby. The birth, regardless of how long or difficult it was, she describes as the most wonderful, joyful and enriching experience of her life.

Within weeks, in a follow-up article, she claims that for the first time in her life she feels emotionally fulfilled and blissfully happy. Despite her short experience of motherhood she feels qualified enough to give advice on the importance of love and bonding; she claims that feeding on demand and having a baby share the marital bed is the only way of true bonding. She and the baby now have a wonderful, often 'spiritual' relationship and understand each other totally. In this short time she also has managed (presumably between two-hourly breast feeds) to fit in a leading part in the next

Oscar Award-winning film, write a best-selling novel, or stage a return to the catwalk, showing the world how easy it is to get back into shape after giving birth.

All this, she claims, is achieved without hired help as she wants the baby to grow up in a normal environment. Yet we never see such a mother struggling to board the number 52 bus, with a bag of Pampers in one hand, several bags of shopping in the other, and the baby hanging in a sling. It is not surprising, with all the pressure created by the media and these 'perfect mothers', that many 'normal mothers' feel very inadequate during the first few weeks. The reality is that for the majority of mothers without paid help, along with the feelings of joy and love, there can be those of sheer exhaustion from nights of broken sleep and feelings of failure and frustration when an irritable baby cannot be calmed. These feelings can lead a mother to believe that she does not love her baby enough or is not bonding properly.

True bonding is something that evolves over many weeks and months. Do not be pressurized into believing that 'demand feeding and sleeping' is the only way to bond with your baby. Time and time again I get calls from depressed mothers who are feeling so guilty and resentful that they are not bonding with their babies. The real problem stems not from the lack of bonding but from the lack of sleep. The truth is that for any normal mother, weeks of sleep deprivation, caused by endless middle-of-the-night feeding, is bound to hamper bonding.

Within a short time of getting the baby into a routine (see Chapter 7) I find the mother's depression and resentfulness disappear. It is much easier to bond with a happy, contented baby, than an irritable, fretful one who needs constant feeding and rocking. My routines will help you understand what your baby's needs really are and to know how to fulfil those needs, making the bonding process a happy and more enjoyable one.

Why follow a routine?

Benefits for your baby

The dozens and dozens of baby care books I have read are all in agreement on one aspect: that in the first few weeks it is impossible to put a small baby into a routine. The implication is that if you even attempt to put your baby in a routine you could seriously damage him. Having successfully spent many years teaching parents how to put their newborns into a routine that results in a happy, thriving, contented baby, I can only assume that the authors of these books have not personally worked with enough babies to know that it is possible.

Parents are always amazed at how easily their baby fits into my routines. Many assume that having a baby in a routine can only be achieved by leaving him to yell until the feed is due, or by leaving him to cry himself to sleep. While this is often the case with the old-fashioned four-hourly feeding pattern, nothing could be further from the truth with my routines.

These routines are created to meet the natural sleep and feeding needs of all healthy, normal young babies. They also allow for the fact that some babies need more sleep than others, and some may be able to go longer between feeds than others. The basis of these routines evolved over years of observing babies in my care. Some babies would develop a feeding pattern very quickly with little prompting, while others would be difficult to feed and settle for many weeks.

The main observations I made from the babies who settled quickly into a pattern were:

* The parents had a positive approach and tried to keep the first couple of weeks as calm as possible.
* Handling of the baby by visitors was kept to a minimum so that the baby felt relaxed and secure in his new surroundings.
* The baby always had regular sleep times in the dark in his nursery.

- The baby was kept awake for a short spell after the day-time feeds.
- When awake, he was stimulated and played with by the parents.
- He was bathed at the same time every evening, then fed, and settled in the dark in his nursery.

Benefits for you

By following my routines you will soon learn whether your baby is crying from hunger, tiredness or boredom. The fact that you are able to understand his needs and meet them quickly and confidently will leave both you and your baby calm and reassured. The usual situation of fretful baby and fraught mother is avoided.

The other big plus for parents following my routines is that they have free time in the evening, to relax and enjoy each other's company. This is usually not possible for parents of demand-fed babies, who seem to be at their most fretful between 6pm and 10pm, and require endless rocking and patting.

Feeding in the first year | 3

Breast feeding

Breast is best and the most natural way to feed your baby, as all the baby experts agree. Some have dedicated complete books to how to do it successfully and the benefits for both mother and baby. Immediately after the birth, midwives encourage new mothers to put the baby straight to the breast, and guide them through the techniques of positioning and latching the baby on. There are also organizations that devote themselves totally to promoting breast feeding and that also provide trained breast-feeding counsellors to support and guide mothers who are experiencing difficulties in the early weeks.

According to various different surveys, it is therefore very surprising that despite all the help and support available to new mothers, only 67 per cent of breast-feeding mothers are still breast feeding their babies at the age of one month, the rest having given up after two to four weeks.

The most common reasons given by mothers for giving up breast feeding are:

- a feeling that they are not producing enough milk
- cracked nipples and pain during feeding
- the baby is discontented and not thriving
- exhaustion due to the baby feeding for hours at a time, often throughout the whole night
- they don't enjoy breast feeding and start to dread feeding times.

I think it is very sad if a mother has to give up for any or all of the first four reasons. If, however, a mother really hates breast feeding, she should not be pressurized into continuing. To quote child-care expert Penelope Leach, 'feeding is only a part of motherhood'. Having observed hundreds of mothers over the last ten years, I would like to reassure any mother who absolutely hates breast feeding that, contrary to some breast-feeding gurus' advice, your baby will not suffer physically or emotionally if you decide to change to formula milk. The most important thing is that you and your baby are happy with what you doing, which is very difficult if you dislike breast feeding. Speaking from personal experience, my own mother only breast fed me for about ten days, and no one could have bonded more than my mother and me. Equally, I have friends who were breast fed for nearly two years, and they cannot stand the sight of their mothers! So if you decide breast feeding is not for you, ignore any criticism, establish bottle feeding and enjoy your baby. Hundreds of thousands of babies every year all over the world are fed exclusively on formula milk, and grow and thrive happily. The reality is that if 'formula' was not a very good substitute for breast feeding when this is either not possible or not working, it would have been banned by the health authorities years ago.

However, I must stress that contrary to the advice you may get from well-meaning grandmas or aunties, bottle feeding does not necessarily guarantee you a more contented baby, or make it easier to put your baby into a routine. Whether your baby is breast fed or bottle fed, it will still take time and perseverance to establish a routine, so do not change your baby's feeding to 'formula' thinking you will achieve instant results. A bottle-fed baby will need as much guidance and help into a routine as a breast-fed one, the only difference being that all the responsibility normally lies with the mother who is breast feeding. This is where my breast-feeding routines can give the best of both worlds to mothers who wish to breast feed, but also want a routine.

I have tried and tested various ways of establishing breast feeding, and the breast-feeding routine I have devised is without doubt the one that has proved the most successful time and time again. The mothers who follow all my guidelines report that within two weeks a definite pattern of sleeping and feeding has emerged, the baby's weight gain is good and, most importantly, the baby is very happy and content. Before I explain how and why my methods work so well, I will briefly discuss the weak points of other methods I have tried, and why I feel these other methods do not always meet a baby's natural feeding and sleeping needs.

Four-hourly routine

Years ago, when hospital birth took over from home birth, women stayed in the maternity unit for up to 10 or 14 days. By the time they left the hospital their babies were often already in a four-hourly feeding pattern. Breast-feeding mothers were encouraged to adopt the same pattern as that of the formula-fed babies. The babies were brought to their mothers for feeding every four hours, a strict 10–15 minutes on each breast was allowed, then the babies were taken back to the nursery. If a baby could not manage to go four hours between feeds, the mother was told she was not producing enough milk to feed her baby, and was advised to top up with formula. I would be a multimillionaire if I had a pound for every granny who has said to me 'My milk dried up the minute I left the hospital'. The reality was that, due to rigid routines and restricted timing of feeds, the mother's milk had started to dry up long before she left the hospital. The trend for bottle feeding became well established in the fifties and sixties, with many mothers not even attempting to breast feed. This trend continued well into the 1970s. Then, as research started to discover more and more information regarding the health benefits of breast feeding, the trend started to swing back to breast feeding again.

The main reasons why strict four-hourly feeding can fail are:

- Six feeds a day in the early days are often not enough to stimulate a good milk supply.
- Babies need to feed little and often in the early days; restricting feeding to six feeds may lead to your baby being short of his daily intake.
- Babies between one week and six weeks usually need at least 30 minutes to reach the hind milk. Hind milk is at least three times higher in fat content than fore milk, and is essential for satisfying your baby's hunger.

Demand feeding

The advice given nowadays is to feed your baby on demand. Mothers are encouraged to let their babies take the lead, allowing the baby to feed as often and for as long as he wants. This way you can be sure that your baby's nutritional needs are always met and that he never goes hungry, as each time your baby empties the breast this signals the breasts to make more milk. When they leave the hospital, many babies are feeding up to 10 or 12 times a day. Mothers are reassured that this is normal for the first few weeks, that things will eventually settle down, and that the baby will start to go longer between feeds.

While I agree totally that the baby should be frequently put to the breast in the early days to stimulate the breast supply, I think the advice so often given, to let the baby suck as long as he wants, is completely wrong. Some very 'sucky' babies would go on for hours, leaving the new mother in agony before breast feeding has hardly even begun. Time and time again I meet mothers who by the end of the first week of breast feeding are hating it. The cry is always the same: exhaustion from the baby feeding for hours at a time, and tender, painful nipples. Even worse, the nipples can often become cracked and bleeding, as a result of not positioning the baby correctly on the breast. In my experience you can show a mother repeatedly the correct way to latch the baby on to the breast, but if she gets absolutely exhausted by constant feeding day and night, it is unlikely that she will have the energy to concentrate properly on the correct positioning of the baby on the breast.

As well as being told they should feed their baby on demand, mothers are also advised to get a lot of rest and eat properly. This advice is totally contradictory and virtually impossible to follow, leaving the mother feeling like a total failure at the onset of breast feeding.

The second problem that I find occurs time and time again when a new mother is feeding on demand is that of the sleepy baby. Very often, these are babies born by Caesarean. The mother is lulled into a false sense of security; she proudly announces that her baby sleeps and feeds well, often going five to six hours between feeds. By the end of the first week, the mother's milk has come in and balanced out to meet the baby's needs. The reality hits home around the tenth day, when these babies perk up and start to look for more food. The mother then has to resort to feeding little and often to satisfy the baby's needs, which leaves many mothers feeling they are on a backward track. The fact is that it is much easier to get a good milk supply going when the milk first comes in. Yet again the term 'demand feeding' is contradictory. It implies that by feeding your baby every time he demands it you can be sure he is getting enough to eat. All too often it is not made clear to the mothers of these sleepy babies that they should be woken every three to four hours to feed. If necessary a little milk should be expressed two or three times a day to encourage a good milk supply, ready for when the baby starts demanding more feeds.

Last but not least, there is yet another very important reason why the term 'demand feeding' is used too loosely. It is that it leads new mothers to believe that feeding several times a night is normal. Not structuring a feeding pattern offers no guarantee that the baby will automatically feed more during the day. Again the advice is that the baby will sort itself out, but mothers are not told that with some babies it may take months! All too often I visit mothers whose babies are feeding so much in the night that when they do wake up for feeds during the day, they tend to be short, small feeds. This leads to a vicious circle of the baby needing to feed more in the night to satisfy its daily needs.

The main reasons why demand feeding can fail are:

- The term 'demand feeding' is used too literally and the baby is fed every time it cries. Mothers are not taught to look for other reasons why the baby may be crying, ie overstimulation or overtiredness.
- A baby who continues to feed 10–12 times a day after the first week will very quickly become exhausted through lack of sleep.
- Exhaustion and stress reduce the mother's milk supply, increasing the baby's need to feed little and often.
- Exhaustion leads to the mother being too tired to concentrate properly on positioning the baby correctly on the breast for any length of time.
- Poor positioning on the breast is the main reason for painful, and often cracked and bleeding nipples.
- A sleepy baby left too long between feeds in the early days reduces the mother's chances of building up a good milk supply.

My methods for successful breast feeding

The key to successful breast feeding is getting off to the right start. All breast-feeding counsellors agree that in order to produce enough milk, it is essential that the breasts are stimulated frequently during the early days. I agree totally with this advice. Years ago, lack of breast stimulation was one of the main reasons breast feeding failed when a strict four-hourly routine was adhered to. It is also the same reason why breast feeding goes wrong with a very sleepy baby.

Little and often during the first few days is the best way to establish breast feeding. I advise all my mothers to start off by offering five minutes each side every three hours, increasing the time by a few minutes each day until the milk comes in. Somewhere between the third and fifth day your milk will be in, and you should have increased the baby's sucking time on the breast to 15–20 minutes. Many babies will get enough milk from the first breast, and be content to go three hours before demanding a feed again.

However, if you find your baby is demanding food long before three hours have passed, he should be offered both breasts at each feed. It is absolutely essential that you make sure he has emptied the first breast totally before putting him to the second breast. If you change breasts too soon he will end up getting too much fore milk, which is one of the main causes of babies never seeming satisfied and suffering from colic. It may take a sleepy baby 20–25 minutes to reach the very important hind milk (which is at least three times fattier than the fore milk) and to empty the breast.

Positioning the baby at the breast

Feeding your baby three-hourly will help build up your milk supply much quicker, and if he is fed enough during the day he will be much more likely to go to sleep for longer periods between feeds in the night. It also avoids the mother becoming too exhausted, which is another major factor in breast feeding going wrong. During the first few days, between 6am and midnight, wake your baby every three hours for short feeds. This will ensure that the feeding gets off to the best possible start, in time for when the milk comes in. As with anything in life, success only comes from building a good foundation. All my mothers who establish three-hourly feeds in the hospital find that by the end of the first week a pattern has emerged, and then very quickly they can adapt their baby's feeding pattern to my first routine.

The first breast-feeding routine not only helps you establish a good milk supply, but will also enable you to learn all your baby's many different needs: hunger, tiredness, boredom, over-stimulation.

The main reasons why my breast-feeding methods are so successful are:

- Waking the baby three-hourly in the first few days for shorter feeds allows the mother's nipples to get used to the baby's sucking gradually. This avoids the nipples becoming too painful or, even worse, cracked and bleeding. It will also help ease the pain of engorgement when the milk comes in.
- Feeding little and often will avoid the baby spending hours sucking on an empty breast trying to satisfy his hunger, which often occurs when a baby is allowed to go longer than three hours between feeds in the first week.
- A newborn baby's tummy is tiny and his daily needs can only be satisfied by feeding little and often. If you feed your baby three-hourly between 6am and midnight, the 'feeding-all-night syndrome' should never occur. Even a very small baby is capable of going one longer spell in between feeds, and following my advice ensures that this will happen at night, not during the day.

- Successful breast feeding can only be achieved if a mother feels relaxed and comfortable. This is impossible if, having just given birth, she becomes exhausted from being awake and feeding all night. Stress and exhaustion in the first few weeks are two of the main reasons why so many mothers give up breast feeding by the end of the first month.

- Newborn babies do not know the difference between day and night. Babies will only learn to associate daytime with feeding and social activities if they are not allowed to sleep for long periods between feeds from 7am to 7pm.

Milk production

Milk let-down reflex

The hormones produced during your pregnancy help prepare your breasts for the production of milk. Once your baby is born and put to the breast to suck, a hormone called oxytocin is released from the pituitary gland at the base of your brain, which sends a 'let-down' signal to the breasts. The muscles supporting the milk glands contract and the milk is pushed down the 15 or 20 milk ducts as the baby sucks. Many women feel a slight tingling in their breasts, and their womb contracting when their milk lets down. These feelings normally disappear within a week or two. You may also experience a let-down when you hear your baby cry, or if you think about him when you are apart. If you get tense or are very stressed, oxytocin is not released, making it difficult for your milk to let down. Therefore it is essential for successful breast feeding that you feel calm and relaxed. This can be helped by preparing everything needed for a feed in advance. Make sure you are sitting comfortably with your back straight, and the baby well supported. Take time to position him on to the breast correctly. Pain caused by incorrect positioning also affects oxytocin being released, which affects the let-down reflex.

Milk composition

The first milk your breasts will produce is called colostrum. It is higher in protein and vitamins and lower in carbohydrate and fat than the mature milk that comes in between the third and fifth day. Colostrum also contains some of your antibodies, which will help your baby resist any infections you may have had. Compared to the mature milk that soon follows, colostrum is much thicker and looks more yellow. By the second to third day the breasts are producing a mixture of colostrum and mature milk. Then somewhere between the third and fifth day the breasts become engorged, and they will feel very hard, tender and often painful to the touch. This is a sign that the mature milk is fully in. The pain is caused not only by the milk coming in, but by the enlargement of the milk glands in the breasts and the increased blood supply to the breasts. When the milk comes in, it is essential to feed your baby little and often. Not only will it help stimulate a good milk supply, but it will help relieve the pain of engorgement. During this time it may be difficult for your baby to latch on to the breast and it may be necessary to express a little milk before feeding. This can be done by placing warm, wet flannels on the breasts and gently expressing a little milk by hand. Many mothers also find some relief by placing the leaves of a chilled cabbage inside their bras between feeds.

Mature milk looks very different from colostrum. It is thinner and looks slightly blue in colour, and its composition also changes during the feed. At the beginning of the feed your baby gets the fore milk, which is high in volume and low in fat. As the feed progresses your baby's sucking will slow down and he will pause for longer between sucks. This is a sign that he is reaching the hind milk. Although he only gets a small amount of hind milk, it is very important that he is left on the breast long enough to reach it. It is this hind milk that will help your baby go longer between feeds. If you transfer him to the second breast before he has totally emptied the first breast, he will be more likely to get two lots of fore milk. This will have a knock-on effect, and leave him feeling hungry again in a couple of hours. Another feed of fore milk will quickly lead to your baby becoming very 'colicky'. While some babies do not get enough to eat from only one breast and need to be put on the second breast, always check that he has completely emptied the first breast before transferring him. By gently squeezing your nipple between your thumb and forefinger, you will be able to check if there is any milk still in the breast. I find that by the end of the first week, by making sure babies are given at least 25 minutes on the first breast, and offered the second breast for 5–15 minutes, I can be sure that they are getting the right balance of fore milk and hind milk. It also ensures that they are content to go between three and four hours before demanding their next feed. If your baby is feeding from both breasts at each feed, always remember to start the next feed on the breast you last fed from, so that you can be sure that each breast is totally emptied every second feed.

In order to encourage a quick and easy let-down and ensure that your baby gets the right balance of fore milk and hind milk, the following guidelines should be followed:

- Make sure that you rest as much as possible between feeds, and that you do not go too long between meals. Also eat small, healthy snacks between meals.
- Prepare in advance everything needed for the feed: a comfortable chair with arms and a straight back and perhaps a footstool. Cushions to support both you and the baby, a drink of water and some soothing music will all help towards a relaxing, enjoyable feed for both of you.
- It is essential that you take your time to position the baby on the breast correctly; poor positioning leads to painful and often cracked, bleeding nipples. This in turn can affect your let-down and result in a poor feed.
- Always make sure your baby has completely emptied the first breast before putting him on the second. It is the small amount of high-fat hind milk at the end of a feed that will help your baby go longer between feeds.

- Not all babies need the second breast in the early days. If your baby has totally emptied the first breast, burp him and change his nappy, then offer him the second breast. If he needs more he will take it. If not, start him off on that breast at the next feed.
- If your baby does feed from the second breast, you should still start on that breast at the next feed. This will ensure that each breast is totally emptied every second feed, thus signalling the breasts to make more milk.
- Once the milk is in and you have built up the time your baby feeds from the breast, it is important that he is on the breast long enough to completely empty it and reach the hind milk. Some babies need up to 30 minutes to completely empty the breast.
- Never, ever allow your baby to suck on an empty breast; this will only lead to very painful nipples.

Expressing

I believe that expressing milk in the early days plays a huge part in determining how successful a mother will be in combining breast feeding while following a routine. In my first book I said that I was convinced that one of the main reasons the majority of my mothers are so successful at breast feeding is because I encourage the use of an electric expressing machine in the very early days. Having spoken to thousands of mothers since its publication, I would go as far as to say that it is virtually impossible to keep a baby in the routines in the early days if the mother does not express.

The simple reason for this is that breast milk is produced on a supply and demand basis. During the very early days, most babies will empty the first breast and some may take a small amount from the second breast. Very few will empty both breasts at this stage. By the end of the second week the milk production balances out and most mothers are producing exactly the amount their baby is demanding. During the

third and fourth week the baby goes through a growth spurt
and demands more milk. That is where a problem often sets
in if you are attempting to put your baby into a routine and
have followed the current advice of not expressing before six
weeks. In order to meet the increased demand for more food
you would more than likely have to go back to feeding
two or three hourly and often twice in the night. This feeding pattern is repeated each time the baby goes through a
growth spurt and often results in the baby being continually
fed just prior to sleep time. This can create the problem of the
wrong sleep association, making it even more difficult to get
the baby back into the routine.

Mothers who express the extra milk they produce in the
very early days will always be producing more than their
baby needs. When their baby goes through a growth spurt
the routine stays intact, because any increased appetite can
immediately be satisfied simply by expressing less milk at the
early morning feeds. Expressing from the very early days can
also help avoid the problem of a low milk supply. However,
if your baby is over one month and you already have the
problem of a low milk supply, by following my plan for
increasing your milk supply you should see a big improvement within six days. For babies under one month following
the expressing times laid out in the routine should be enough
to increase your supply.

If you have previously experienced difficulties with
expressing do not be disheartened. Expressing at the times
suggested in my routines or the plan on pages 52–5 along
with the following guidelines should help make it easier:

• The best time to express is in the morning as the breasts
  are usually fuller. Expressing will also be easier if done at
  the beginning of a feed. Either express one breast just prior
  to feeding your baby, or feed your baby from one breast,
  then express from the second breast before offering him
  the remainder of his feed. Some mothers actually find that
  expressing is easier when done while they are feeding the
  baby on the other breast. It is also important to note that

expressing at the beginning of a feed allows slightly longer for that breast to make more milk for the next feed.

In my routines I suggest that the mother expresses at 6.45am. However, if you are producing a lot of milk and can't face the early morning slot you could move the expressing of the second breast to around 7.30am after the baby has fed from the first breast. A mother who is concerned about her milk supply or who is following the plan for increasing the milk (on page 52) should try to stick to the recommended times.

- In the early days, you will need to allow at least 15 minutes to express 60–90ml (2–3oz) at the morning feeds, and up to 30 minutes at the evening expressing times. Try to keep expressing times quiet and relaxed. The more you practise the easier it will become. I usually find that by the end of the first month the majority of my mothers can easily express 60–90ml (2–3oz) within five minutes at the morning feeds and 180–240ml (6–8oz) within 10 minutes when using a double pumping system at the 10pm feed.

- An electrical, heavy-duty pumping machine, the type used in hospitals, is by far the best way to express milk in the early days. The suction of these machines is designed to simulate a baby's sucking rhythm, encouraging the milk flow. If you are expressing both breasts at 10pm it is also worthwhile investing in an attachment that enables both breasts to be expressed at once, therefore reducing the time spent expressing.

- Sometimes the let-down is slower in the evening when the breasts are producing less milk; a relaxing warm bath or shower will often help encourage the milk to flow more easily. Also gently massaging the breasts before and during expressing will help.

- Some mothers find that it is helpful to have a picture of their baby close by for them to look at, while others find it better to watch a favourite television programme or to chat to their partners or husbands. Experiment with different approaches to see which one works best for you.

Plan for increased milk supply

Days one to three

6.45am
- Express 30ml (1oz) from each breast.
- Baby should be awake, and feeding no later than 7am regardless of how often he fed in the night.
- He should be offered 20–25 minutes on the fullest breast, then 10–15 on the second breast.
- Do not feed after 7.45am. He can stay awake for up to two hours.

8am
- It is very important that you have a breakfast of cereal, toast and a drink no later than 8am.

9am
- If your baby has not been settling well for his nap offer him 5–10 minutes on the breast from which he was last fed.
- Try to have a short rest when the baby is sleeping.

10am
- Baby must be fully awake now, regardless of how long he slept.
- He should be given 20–25 minutes from the breast he last fed on while you drink a glass of water and have a small snack.
- Express 60ml (2oz) from the second breast, and then offer him 10–20 minutes on the same breast.

11.45am
- He should be given the 60ml (2oz) that you expressed to ensure that he does not wake up hungry during his midday nap.
- It is very important that you have a good lunch and a rest before his next feed.

2pm
- Baby should be awake and feeding no later than 2pm, regardless of how long he has slept.

- Give him 20–25 minutes from the breast he last fed on while you drink a glass of water. Express 60ml (2oz) from the second breast, and then offer him 10–20 minutes on the same breast.

4pm
- Baby will need a short nap according to the routine appropriate for his age.

5pm
- Baby should be fully awake and feeding no later than 5pm.
- Give 15–20 minutes from both breasts.

6.15pm
- Baby should be offered a top-up feed of expressed milk from the bottle. A baby under 8 lb in weight will probably settle with 60–90ml (2–3oz), bigger babies may need 120–150ml (4–5oz).
- Once your baby is settled it is important that you have a good meal and a rest.

8pm
- Express from both breasts.

10pm
- It is important that you express from both breasts at this time, as the amount you get will be a good indicator of how much milk you are producing.
- Arrange for your husband or another family member to give the late feed to the baby so you can have an early night.

10.30pm
- Baby should be awake and feeding no later than 10.30pm. He can be given a full feed of either formula or expressed milk from a bottle. Refer to the chart on page 63 for details of the amounts to give.

In the night
- A baby who has had a full feed from the bottle at 10.30pm should manage to get to 2–2.30am in the morning. He

should then be offered 20–25 minutes from the first breast, then 10–15 minutes from the second. In order to avoid a second waking in the night at 5am it is very important that he feeds from both breasts.

- If all is well with your baby at 10.30pm, yet he still wakes earlier than 2am, the cause may not be hunger. The following checklist gives other reasons which may be causing him to wake earlier:
  - Kicking off the covers may be the cause of your baby waking earlier than 2am. A baby under six weeks who wakes up thrashing around may still need to be fully swaddled. A baby over six weeks may benefit from being half swaddled under the arms in a thin cotton sheet. With all babies it is important to ensure that the top sheet is tucked in well, down the sides and at the bottom of the cot.
  - The baby should be fully awake at the 10pm feed. With a baby who is waking up before 2am it may be worthwhile keeping him awake longer, and offering him some more milk just before you settle him at around 11.30pm.

Day four

By day four, your breasts should be feeling fuller in the morning and the following alteration should be made to the above plan.

- If your baby is sleeping well between 9am and 9.45am, reduce the time on the breast at 9am to five minutes.
- The top-up at 11.45 can be reduced by 30 ml (1 oz) if he is sleeping well at lunch time, or shows signs of not feeding well at the 2pm feed.
- The expressing at the 2pm feed should be dropped, which should mean your breasts are fuller by the 5pm feed.
- If you feel your breasts are fuller at 5pm, make sure he totally empties the first breast before putting him onto the second breast. If he has not emptied the second breast before his bath he should be offered it again after the bath, and before he is given a top-up.

- The 8pm expressing should be dropped and the 10pm expressing brought forward to 9.30pm. It is important that both breasts are completely emptied at the 9.30pm expressing.

Day five

- Dropping the 2pm and 8pm expressing on the fourth day should result in your breasts being very engorged on the morning of the fifth day; it is very important that the extra milk is totally emptied at the first feed in the morning.
- At the 7am feed the baby should be offered 20–25 minutes on the fullest breast, then 10–15 minutes on the second after you have expressed. The amount you will express will depend on the weight of your baby, as it is important that you take just the right amount so that enough is left for your baby to get a full feed. If you have managed to express a minimum of 120ml (4oz) at the 10pm feed, then you should manage to express the following amounts:
  a) baby weighing 8–10lb – express 120ml (4oz)
  b) baby weighing 10–12lb – express 90ml (3oz)
  c) baby weighing over 12lb – express 60ml (2oz)

Day six

By the sixth day, your milk supply should have increased enough for you to drop all top-up feeds, and follow the routine appropriate for your baby's age. It is very important that you also follow the guidelines for expressing as set out in the routines. This will ensure that you will be able to satisfy your baby's increased appetite during his next growth spurt. I would also suggest that you continue with one bottle of either expressed or formula milk at the 10pm feed until your baby is weaned onto solids at four months. This will allow the feed to be given by your husband or partner, enabling you to get to bed earlier, which in turn will make it easier for you to cope with the middle of the night feed.

Weaning your baby from the breast to the bottle

However long you have breast fed, it is important to plan the transition from breast feeding to bottle feeding properly. When deciding for how long you intend to breast feed your baby, you should take into consideration that once you have established a good milk supply, you must allow approximately a week to drop each feed. For example, it can take six weeks to establish a good milk supply, and if you decide to give up breast feeding, you should allow at the very least a further five weeks to drop all breast feeds and establish bottle feeding. This information is very important for mothers who are planning to go back to work. If you give up breast feeding before you have established a good milk supply, you should still allow enough time for your baby to get used to feeding from the bottle. Some babies can get very upset if they suddenly lose the pleasure and comfort they get from breast feeding.

For a mother who has breast fed for less than a month, I generally advise a period of three to four days in between dropping feeds. For a mother who has been breast feeding longer than a month, it is best to allow five to seven days in between dropping feeds. Assuming that the baby is already on a bottle feed at 10pm, the next breast feed to drop should be at 11am. The best way to do this is gradually to reduce the length of time the baby feeds from the breast by five minutes each day and top up with formula. Once your baby is taking a full bottle feed the breast feed can be dropped. If you plan the weaning carefully from the breast to formula, your baby will have time to adjust to the bottle and you avoid the risk of developing mastitis. This can happen if the milk ducts become blocked due to engorgement – a common problem among mothers who instantly drop a feed.

I suggest that you continue to express at 10pm throughout the weaning process. The amount of milk expressed will be an indicator of how quickly your milk supply is going down.

Some mothers find that once they are down to two breast feeds a day their milk reduces very rapidly. The signs to watch out for are: your baby being irritable and unsettled after a feed or wanting a feed long before it is normally due. If your baby shows either of these signs he should be topped up immediately after the breast feed with 30–60ml (1–2oz) of expressed milk or formula. This will ensure that his sleeping pattern does not go wrong due to hunger.

The chart below is a guideline for which feeds to drop first. Each stage represents the period of time between dropping feeds, either three to four days or five to seven days, depending on how long you have been breast feeding.

Time of feeds	7am	11am	2.30pm	6.30pm	10.30pm
Stage one	Breast	Formula	Breast	Breast	Express*
Stage two	Breast	Formula	Formula	Breast	Express
Stage three	Breast	Formula	Formula	Formula	Express
Stage four	Breast	Formula	Formula	Formula	
Stage five	Formula	Formula	Formula	Formula	

* I recommend that mothers should continue to express at the 10.30pm feed until the baby is three to four months old. This helps maintain a good milk supply, and can be used as an approximate gauge of how much milk they are producing. I find that a mother will usually produce overnight roughly twice the amount she has expressed. When you reach Stage Three of the weaning process, the 10.30pm expressing should be dropped gradually, reducing the expressing time by three minutes each night. Once you are only expressing 60ml (2oz) and going comfortably through the night, the expressing can be dropped altogether. When the last breast feed has been dropped, care should be taken not to stimulate the breasts. Sitting in a warm bath with the water covering the breasts helps to get rid of any small amount of milk remaining in the breasts without stimulating them to make more.

Your questions answered

Q I have very small breasts and am worried that I may not be able to produce enough milk to satisfy my baby's needs.

A • Breast size is totally irrelevant when it comes to producing breast milk. Each breast, regardless of shape or size, has 15–20 ducts, each duct with its own cluster of milk-making cells. Milk is made within these cells and pushed down the ducts when the baby sucks.

• During the early days make sure your baby is put to the breast frequently. Most babies need a minimum of eight feeds a day to help stimulate the breasts and establish a good milk supply.

• Always make sure that your baby totally empties the first breast before putting him on the second breast. This signals the breast to make more milk and also ensures that your baby gets the important hind milk, which is much fattier than the fore milk.

Q My friend was in agony when her milk came in. Is there anything I can do to help relieve the pain of engorgement?

A • Put your baby to the breast often and do not let him go longer than three hours during the day between feeds or four to five hours at night.

• A warm bath or warm wet flannels placed on the breasts before a feed will help the milk flow and, if need be, gently expressing a little milk by hand will make it easier for the baby to latch on.

• Damp flannels chilled in the fridge and placed on the breasts after a feed will help constrict the blood vessels and reduce the swelling.

• Take the leaves from just under the outer leaves of a cabbage, chill in the fridge and place on your breasts inside your bra between feeds.

• Wear a well-fitting nursing bra that supports your breasts. Make sure that it is not too tight under the arms and does not flatten your nipples.

Q Many of my friends had to give up breast feeding because it was so painful.

A • The main reason women experience pain in the early days is because the baby is not positioned on the breast correctly. The baby ends up chewing on the end of the nipple, causing much pain for the mother, and more often than not resulting in cracked, bleeding nipples and a poor feed for the baby. A pattern soon emerges of the baby needing to feed very quickly again, giving him even more opportunity to damage the nipples.

- Make sure that you always hold your baby with his tummy to your tummy and that his mouth is open wide enough for him to take all of the nipple and as much of the areola as he can manage into his mouth. Apart from ensuring that your baby is well positioned, it is important that you are sitting comfortably. The ideal chair should have a straight back, preferably with arms so that you can position a cushion to support the arm in which you are holding the baby. If you do not support your arm it will be much more difficult to position and support your baby properly. This can cause him to pull on the breast, which will be painful for you.

Q I have a three-week-old baby and I am getting very confused over the conflicting advice. Some people say give both breasts at each feed, others say one is enough.

A • Be guided by your baby. If he feeds from one breast, is content to go three to four hours between feeds, and is putting on 6–8oz in weight each week, one breast is obviously enough.

- If he is looking for food after two hours or is waking up in the night more than once, it would be advisable to offer him the second breast. You may find he only needs the second breast later in the day when your milk supply is at its lowest.

- Whether your baby has one or two breasts at a feed, always check that the first breast is completely empty before putting him on the second. This can be done by gently squeezing the area around the nipple between your thumb and forefinger.

Q Do I need to avoid certain foods while breast feeding?

A • You should continue with the same varied healthy diet that you followed throughout your pregnancy. In addition, you should include small healthy snacks between meals to help keep your energy levels up.

- Ensure that you eat at least 180g (6oz) of either poultry, lean meat or fish. Vegetarians should eat the equivalent in beans, pulses and rice, etc. I have noticed that on the days when some of my breast-feeding mothers did not eat enough protein, their babies were much more unsettled.

- Some research points to dairy products as the cause of colic in certain babies. If you find your baby develops colic, it may be wise to discuss how to monitor your dairy intake with your health visitor or paediatrician.

- Alcohol, artificial sweeteners and caffeine should be avoided. Remember that caffeine is not only found in coffee but also in tea, soft drinks and chocolate. I have found all of these things can upset most babies.

- Strawberries, tomatoes, mushrooms, onions and fruit juice if taken in large quantities have left many of my babies very irritable. While I do not suggest cutting out all of these from your diet, I would suggest you keep a record of any food or drink consumed 12–16 hours prior to your baby showing signs of tummy ache, explosive bowel movements, excessive wind and crying fits.

- While working in the Middle and Far East I observed that breast-feeding mothers followed a much blander diet than normal and highly spiced foods were omitted. Perhaps it would be wise to avoid curries in the early days.

- Although it is advisable to avoid alcohol, especially spirits, while breast feeding, some experts advise that a small glass of wine or a Guinness can be beneficial to a mother who is finding it hard to unwind in the evening.

Q My two-week-old baby wakes up yelling for a feed, only to fall asleep after five minutes on the breast. She then demands to be fed two hours later, leaving me absolutely exhausted.

A • Always make sure your baby is fully awake before you
     attempt to feed him. Unwrap him in the cot, take his
     legs out of his baby-grow and allow the cool air to get
     to his skin and give him time to wake up by himself.
   • It is very important that sleepy babies are kept cool
     while feeding. He should not be overdressed and the
     room should not be too warm. Have a play mat next to
     you on the floor and the minute he gets sleepy, put
     him on the play mat. If necessary remove his baby-
     grow, as this will encourage him to stretch and kick.
     Within a few minutes he will probably protest about
     being put down, so pick him up and give him a few
     more minutes on the same breast. This procedure often
     has to be repeated two or three times. Once he has had
     20 minutes on the first breast, burp him well and
     change his nappy. He can then be put back on the first
     breast if he has not emptied it, or transferred to the
     second.
   • If you are not using formula at the 10.30pm feed, it is
     also a good idea to express some milk early in the morn-
     ing and get your partner to do the 10–11pm feed. This
     way you will at least manage to get an uninterrupted
     few hours' sleep for one part of the night.

Bottle feeding

Many mothers believe if they bottle feed their babies it will
be easier to get them into a routine. The reality is that bottle
feeding alone is no guarantee of a happy, contented baby. A
formula-fed baby will need as much guidance into a routine
as a breast-fed one. When I do my consultations, I find I have
as many bottle-feeding mothers requesting advice as I have
breast-feeding mothers. Being woken up several times a night
is exhausting, regardless of how you are feeding your baby.
The fact that someone else can give a bottle feed is often
quoted as being an advantage, but this can also be possible

for a breast-feeding mother who is expressing in the morning. The one real advantage that bottle feeding does have over breast feeding is that you do not need to worry about what you eat or drink.

If you have decided to bottle feed, the same routines as for breast feeding should be followed. The only difference is that you may find your baby is happy to go longer than three hours after the 7am feed, otherwise the timing is exactly the same. In the instances where a feed is being split, ie one breast before the bath and one after, the same pattern applies to bottle feeding. I would normally make up two separate smaller feeds for this time.

How much and how often

Health authorities advise that a baby under four months would need 75ml (2½oz) of milk for each pound of his body weight; a baby weighing around 7lb would need approximately 530ml (18oz) a day. That amount would be divided into six feeds a day. This is only a guideline; hungrier babies may need an extra ounce at some feeds. If your baby is one of these try to ensure that you structure your feeds so he is taking the bigger feeds at the right time, ie 7am, 10.30am or 10.30pm. If you allow him to get into the habit of having bigger feeds in the middle of the night, it would eventually have the knock-on effect of him being not so hungry when he wakes in the morning. A vicious circle emerges where he needs to feed in the night because he does not feed enough during the day.

The same guidelines apply as for breast feeding: aim to get the baby to take most of his daily milk requirements between 7am and 11pm. This way he will only need a small feed in the middle of the night, and will eventually drop it altogether.

The chart on page 63 is an example of the feeding pattern of one of my babies during his first month. He weighed 7lb at birth and, with a weekly gain of 6–8oz, reached just over 9lb when he was one month old. By structuring the feeding (the bigger feeds at the right times) he was well on the way to dropping his middle-of-the-night feed, and at six weeks he was sleeping through to 6.30am.

Times	7am	10–10.30am	2–2.30pm	5pm	6.15pm	10–11pm	2–3am	Totals
Week 1	90ml (3oz)	90ml (3oz)	90ml (3oz)	60ml (2oz)	60ml (2oz)	90ml (3oz)	90ml (3oz)	570ml (19oz)
Week 2	90ml (3oz)	120ml (4oz)	90ml (3oz)	90ml (3oz)	60ml (2oz)	120ml (4oz)	90ml (3oz)	660ml (22oz)
Week 3	120ml (4oz)	120ml (4oz)	90ml (3oz)	90ml (3oz)	90ml (3oz)	120ml (4oz)	90ml (3oz)	720ml (24oz)
Week 4	150ml (5oz)	120ml (4oz)	120ml (4oz)	90ml (3oz)	90ml (3oz)	150ml (5oz)	60ml (2oz)	780ml (26oz)

N.B. These daily amounts of milk in the chart were calculated to suit that particular baby's specific needs. Remember to adjust the quantities of milk to suit your baby's own needs, but still follow the feeding times of the chart. During growth spurts make sure that the 7am, 10.30am and 10–11pm feeds are the first to be increased.

Establishing bottle feeding

When your baby is born, the hospital will provide you with ready-made formula. You may be given a choice of two different brands; both are approved by the health authorities and there is very little difference in the composition of either milk. The bottles of formula will come with pre-packed sterilized teats, which are used once and then thrown away. Unless the jars have been stored in the fridge they do not need to be heated; they can be given at room temperature. However, if for some reason you do decide to heat the formula, do so by using either an electric bottle warmer or by standing it in a jug of boiling water.

Never heat up the formula in a microwave, as the heat may not be evenly distributed and you could end up by scalding your baby's mouth. Whichever form of heating you use, always test the temperature before giving the bottle to your baby. This can be done by shaking a few drops on the inside of your wrist; it should feel lukewarm, never hot. Once milk is heated, it should never be reheated as this very rapidly increases the bacteria levels in the milk, which is one of the main causes of upset tummies in formula-fed babies.

The advice given in hospital for formula-fed babies seems to be much the same as that for breast-fed babies: 'Feed on demand whenever the baby wants and however much he wants'. While you do not have the problem of establishing a milk supply as in breast feeding, many of the other problems are likely to occur. A bottle fed baby weighing 7lb or more at birth could go straight on to the two- to four-week routine. A smaller baby might not manage to last quite as long between feeds and need feeding nearer three-hourly.

Ready-made formula is incredibly expensive to use all the time; most parents only use it on outings or in emergencies. Before leaving the hospital, arrange for someone to buy at least two large tins of powdered formula milk of the same brand as the ready-made milk to which your baby has been introduced at the hospital.

Once home, you will get into a routine of making up in advance the feeds needed for the next 24 hours. When making up the formula, choose a quiet time of the day when you are not too tired and follow the instructions on the tin very carefully. Any feeds left over from the previous day should be discarded; likewise never save unfinished feeds. After a feed has been heated up it should be used within one hour and any remaining after this time should be thrown out and, if necessary, a fresh feed heated up. In the early days it is advisable to have an extra bottle of boiled water in the fridge, ready for emergencies. Water left out of the fridge should be okay provided it is used within a few hours. However, if the weather is hot I would not leave it out for long.

Hygiene and sterilization

The utmost attention must be paid to hygiene: the sterilizing of all your baby's feeding equipment and the preparation and storing of his formula milk.

The area where you sterilize and prepare your baby's formula should be kept spotlessly clean. Every morning the work-top should be thoroughly washed down with hot soapy water, the cloth used should then be rinsed well under hot running water and the surface wiped again to remove any traces of soap. This should be followed by a final wipe-down using kitchen roll and antiseptic spray.

The guidelines below, if applied to the letter, will reduce the risk of germs, which are so often the cause of tummy upsets in very young babies.

- Surfaces should be washed down thoroughly every day as described above.
- After each feed the bottle and teat should be rinsed out thoroughly using cold water, and put aside in a bowl ready for washing and sterilizing.
- Get into the habit of sterilizing and preparing feeds at the same time every day. Choose a time when you are not too tired and are able to concentrate properly. Most of my mothers find that 12 noon, when the baby has gone for his long nap, is a good time.
- Hands should always be washed thoroughly with anti-bacterial soap under warm running water, then dried with kitchen roll, not a kitchen towel, which is a breeding ground for germs.
- A separate kettle should be kept for boiling the baby's water; this avoids the water accidentally being boiled a second time if someone wants to make a cup of tea.
- Every day empty the kettle and rinse it out. The water from the tap should be allowed to run for a couple of minutes before filling the kettle.
- Boil the water first, so that it has time to cool while you are washing and sterilizing the bottles.
- Throw away any feeds in the fridge left over from the previous 24 hours.
- Fill the bowl in which the dirty bottles are stored with hot, soapy water. Using a long-handled bottle brush carefully

scrub all the bottles, rims, caps and teats inside and out. Particular attention should be given to the necks and rims. Then under a hot running tap carefully rinse everything. Wash and rinse the bowl thoroughly, then place all the equipment in the bowl under the running hot water tap. This is to check that everything is thoroughly rinsed – the water should run clear.

- The sterilizer should be rinsed out every day, and the removable parts checked and, if necessary, washed and rinsed. The bottles and teats should then be packed into the sterilizer following the manufacturer's instructions.

- When the water in the kettle is cool and the bottles sterilized, carefully follow the instructions on the tin of formula and make up enough feeds for the next 24 hours. In the early days make up an extra bottle of boiled water for emergencies. Once made up, formula should be put immediately into the fridge.

Giving the feed

Prepare everything in advance: chair, cushions, bib and muslin. As with breast feeding, it is important that you are sitting comfortably (see page 7), and in the early days I advise all mothers to support the arm in which they are holding the baby with a pillow, which enables you to keep the baby on a slight slope with his back straight. By holding the baby as shown in diagram A (opposite), you will lessen the likelihood of your baby getting air trapped in his tummy if fed as shown in diagram B.

Before starting to feed, loosen and screw the teat back on; it should be very slightly loose. If it is screwed on too tightly it will not allow air into the bottle, and your baby will end up sucking and not getting any milk.

Check also that the milk is not too hot; it should be just slightly warm. If you get your baby used to very warm milk, you will find that as the feed progresses and the milk gets cool he will refuse to feed. As it is dangerous to reheat the milk or keep the milk standing in hot water for any length of

*Positioning of your baby while
bottle feeding*

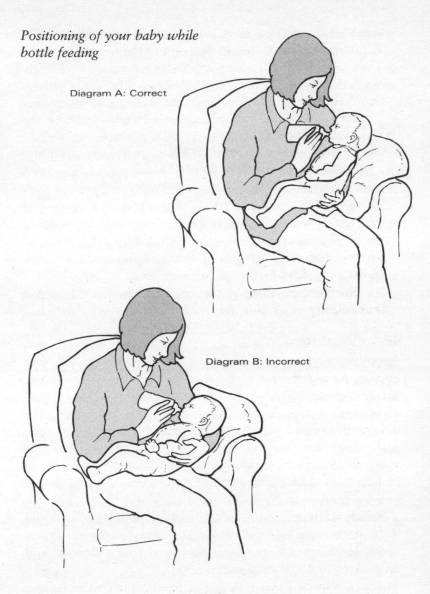

Diagram A: Correct

Diagram B: Incorrect

time, you could end up having to heat up two bottles for
every feed.

Once feeding, make sure that the bottle is kept tilted up far
enough to ensure that the teat is always filled with milk, to

prevent your baby taking in too much air. Allow your baby to drink as much as he wants before stopping to burp him. If you try to burp him before he is ready he will only get very cross and upset.

Some babies will take most of their feed, burp and then want a break of 10–15 minutes before finishing the remainder of the milk. In the early days, allowing for a break midway, it can take up to 40 minutes to give the bottle. Once your baby is six to eight weeks old he will most likely finish his feed in about 20 minutes.

If you find your baby is taking a very long time to feed or keeps falling asleep half-way through a feed, it could be because the hole in the teat is too small. I find that many of my babies have to go straight on to a medium-flow teat as the slow-flow one is too slow.

Occasionally there are babies who will drink a full feed in 10–15 minutes and look for more. These babies are often referred to as 'hungrier babies'; the reality is that these babies are usually 'sucky' babies, not hungrier ones. Because they have such a strong suck they are able to finish the bottle very quickly. Sucking is not only a means of feeding for a baby, but in the early days one of their natural pleasures. If your baby is taking the required amount of formula at each feed very quickly, and looking for more, it may be worthwhile trying a teat with a smaller hole. Offering him a dummy after feeds may also help satisfy his 'sucking needs'.

It is very easy for bottle-fed babies to gain weight too quickly if they are allowed to have feeds well in excess of the amounts recommended for their weight. While a few ounces a day extra should not create a problem, a baby who is overeating and regularly putting on more than 8oz each week, will eventually become too fat and reach a stage where milk alone is not enough to satisfy his hunger. If this happens before the recommended age for giving solids, it can create a real problem.

For establishing successful bottle feeding the following guidelines should be observed:

- Before beginning the feed, check that the ring holding the teat and the bottle together is very slightly loose; if it is too tight it will restrict the flow of the milk.
- Check that the milk is the right temperature; it should be lukewarm, not hot.
- To avoid wind problems, which are very common among formula-fed babies, always make sure that you are comfortable and holding your baby correctly before beginning the feed.
- Some very young babies need a break in the middle of the feed. Allow up to 40 minutes for your baby to take a full feed.
- If you find you are having always to wake your baby for the 7am feed, only to find he is not so hungry then, cut back the middle-of-the-night feed by 30ml (1oz).
- During growth spurts make sure that you follow the guidelines in the next section. This will avoid your baby cutting back, or even dropping, the wrong feeds first.

Understanding your baby's sleep | 4

Sleep is probably the most misunderstood and confusing aspect of parenthood. The misconception is that for the first few weeks, all the baby will do is feed and sleep. While many do, the fact that there are over 126 sleep clinics in the United Kingdom specially for babies and children is proof that a great many do not. If your newborn or young baby is one of the latter, tense, fretful and difficult to settle, please take heart as this need not be a reflection of your baby's future sleep habits.

Accomplishing a regular sleep pattern can be achieved without distress to you or your baby by observing the guidelines I have laid out in this book for your baby's routine. By being patient, consistent and allowing time for my routine to be established, you can avoid the agony of months of sleepless nights that so many parents go through. It has worked for hundreds of my babies and their parents, so it can work for you!

The golden rule, if you want your baby to sleep through the night from an early age and ensure a long-term healthy sleep pattern, is to establish the right associations and structure your baby's feeds from the day you arrive home from the hospital. The advice given in most of the baby books and by hospital staff is that newborn babies should feed on demand as often and for as long as they need. You will be told to accept that your baby's erratic sleeping and feeding patterns are normal and that things will improve by three months of age. I receive endless phone calls and letters from distraught mothers whose infants aged anywhere between three months and three years have serious sleep and feeding problems, which continually disproves the theory that babies will put themselves into a routine by three months. Even if a baby does do this, it is unlikely to be a routine that fits in with the rest of the family.

While some experts would agree that some babies are capable of sleeping through the night by three months, they do not stress the importance of guiding the baby towards this goal. The innocent and weary mother believes in a miraculous improvement at three months, but this is unlikely to happen if her baby has not learned the difference between day and night, naps and the long sleep, and if the parent has not learned how to structure feeds which need to be established from day one.

Sleep and demand feeding

The phrase 'demand feeding' is used time and time again, misleading a new mother into believing that any sort of routine in the early days could deny her baby nutritionally and, according to some experts, emotionally. While I would agree totally that the old-fashioned four-hourly routine of feeding, whether breast or bottle, is not natural to newborn babies, I feel the term 'feeding on demand' is used too loosely. All too often I get desperate telephone calls from the maternity wards. The cry for help is nearly always the same. The baby is feeding up to an hour at a time, usually two hourly from 6pm until 5am. The mother is usually exhausted and starting to suffer from cracked nipples.

When I ask what the baby is like during the day the usual reply is: 'He's ever so good during the day; he will feed then go four hours or longer.' The experts are forever telling us that a newborn baby can need as many as 8 to 12 feeds a day. It is not surprising then that a baby who has only four or even fewer feeds between 6am and 6pm is going to wake up many times in the night to satisfy his daily needs. Despite the advice that newborns need so many feeds in the day, it never ceases to amaze me that hospital staff actually encourage new mothers to let their babies sleep for long spells in the day to prepare them for the tough night ahead. The pattern for sleepless nights unfortunately is often set before mother and baby leave the hospital.

Once home, new parents become totally exhausted as they start to experience more and more difficulty in settling the baby. In desperation they follow the advice given in nearly all the current baby books available, ie rock the baby to sleep, feed the baby to sleep, drive the baby round in the car until he falls asleep, and if all else fails take the baby into bed.

It is generally accepted by most of the baby experts that the behaviour of the baby is normal and that this way of dealing with the problem is normal. After months of sleepless nights and exhausting days with the baby still feeding two or three hourly, many parents ask their GP to refer them to a baby sleep clinic. Or they purchase one or several of the many books on how to get your baby to sleep through the night, only to be told they got it all wrong in the first place. The real reason their baby is unable to sleep well is because he has the wrong associations with going to sleep, ie feeding, rocking, patting, etc.

Dilly Dawes, a leading child psychotherapist with the Tavistock Clinic, and David Messer at the University of Herefordshire have both done extensive research into the sleeping patterns of babies and young children. Both come to the same conclusion, that a baby's sleeping habits can be determined by the prenatal expectations of the mother. Dilly describes mothers as either 'regulators' or 'facilitators'. The regulator mother has very clear ideas about how the baby should fit into her life. The facilitator mother tries to adapt to suit her baby's inclinations. Dilly claims that regulators are less likely to have problems than facilitators. David Messer seems to back this up. He claims that if a mother expects to get up several times a night, she probably will.

My own experience finds this behaviour to be true of

many parents. But the facilitator mother's attitude will often change once she fully understands that her baby is unable to sleep well because of the wrong associations he has learnt from her in order to get to sleep. In order to get these associations correct, it is important that you establish whether your baby is really ready to sleep. An understanding of the natural sleep rhythms of very young babies is essential, otherwise you will be fighting a losing battle.

Sleep rhythms

Most of the leading experts would agree that a newborn baby will sleep approximately 16 hours a day in the first few weeks. This sleep is broken up into a series of short and longer sleeps. In the early days sleep is very much linked to the baby's need to feed little and often. It can take well up to an hour to feed, burp and change the baby, after which time he falls quickly into a deep sleep, often sleeping through to the next feed. It is easy to see why new parents get lulled into a false sense of security. The baby does exactly what the text books say. Over a 24-hour period, with six to eight feeds a day lasting between 45 minutes and one hour, the baby ends up sleeping approximately 16 hours a day.

Usually between the third and fourth week, the baby becomes more alert, and will not fall straight into a deep sleep after feeding. The anxious parents, believing that the baby should fall asleep straight after feeding, start to resort to some or all of the methods mentioned earlier. They do not realize that the behaviour of the baby is totally normal.

It is around this age that the different stages of sleep become more apparent. Like adults, babies go through different stages of sleep. They drift from light sleep into a dream-like sleep known as REM sleep, then into a deep sleep. The cycle is much shorter than that of an adult, lasting approximately 45 minutes to one hour. While some babies only stir when they drift into light sleep, others will wake up fully. If the baby is due for a feed, this does not create a problem. However, if it is only one hour since the baby fed, and the baby does not learn to settle himself, a real problem can develop over the months ahead.

Recent research has shown that all babies drift into light sleep and wake up approximately the same number of times during the night. Only the poor sleepers are unable to drift back into deep sleep, because they are used to being helped to sleep by one or all of the methods mentioned earlier.

If you want your baby to develop good sleep habits from an early age it is important to avoid the wrong sleep assocations. My routines are structured so that your baby feeds well, never gets overtired, and does not learn the wrong assocations when going to sleep.

Early-morning waking

I have always believed that whether a child becomes an early morning waker is very much determined by what happens during the first year. In order to avoid this problem it is crucial that the baby sleeps in a very dark room and that the mother treats any feeds before 7am like night-time feeds. They should be done with the minimum of fuss, with no talking or eye contact and the baby should be settled back to sleep until 7.30am.

This approach has worked for the hundreds of babies I have helped care for, none of which ever got up before 7am, once they were sleeping through the night. Certainly some of them would waken around 5–6am, and perhaps chatter or sing for a short spell, before returning to sleep.

Since the publication of the first edition of this book and my other books I have spoken to hundreds of parents who have experienced problems with early-morning waking, and a further reason for early-morning wakings has become very apparent. One thing that nearly all these parents had in common is that they did not follow my advice in the routines of allowing their babies to wake up naturally. Most admitted to picking their babies up the minute they started to wake up from day-time naps. I believe that over a period of time it is not surprising that these babies came to expect the same thing to happen when they woke early in the morning.

Somewhere between 8 and 12 weeks the majority of babies do not wake up from naps immediately looking for food. This is a good time to encourage them to lie in their cot for a short time after waking. I am convinced that by doing this, along with the guidelines listed below, there will be less chance of your baby becoming an early-morning waker.

- Research shows that the chemicals in the brain work differently in the dark, preparing it for sleep. Get your baby used to sleeping in a very dark room from day one, with the door shut. Check that their are no chinks of light at the top of the curtains or the sides. Even the smallest amount of light can be enough to waken the baby fully when he comes into a light sleep.
- Until they reach 6 months the 'Moro reflex' can be quite strong with some babies and is very obvious in the early days. The baby flings his arms and legs back in jerky movements, usually if he gets shocked, startled by a sudden loud noise or being put down too roughly or too quickly. Hence the reason that the Moro reflex is more often referred to as the 'startle reflex'.

   As the weeks go by and the baby becomes more relaxed, the Moro reflex is less frequent. But it can take up to seven to eight months before it disappears altogether. I have observed many babies coming into their light sleep in the middle of the night and thrashing their legs up and down hysterically because they have kicked off their covers.

   For this reason I believe it is very important that a baby is tucked in very securely by his bed covers until the Moro reflex has totally disappeared. The sheet and blankets should be placed lengthways across the width of the cot and then two rolled hand towels pushed down between the spars and the mattress to prevent this happening (see page 5). For babies who still manage to work their way up the cot, a very lightweight sleeping bag of no more than 0.5 tog can be used, along with being tucked in with a cotton sheet.

- If your baby is feeding at 5–6am, treat it like a night feed. It should be done as quickly as possible in a dimly lit room without any eye contact or talking. Only change his nappy if really necessary.

- Do not drop the 10pm feed until your baby has reached four months and has started on solids. If he goes through a growth spurt before he starts his solids, he can be offered extra milk at this feed. This reduces the chances of him waking early due to hunger.

The following extract is written by a mother I worked with and shows how problems arise and how they can be dealt with.

Before William was born I had been warned that I should always let baby fall asleep from feeding, and had also had some good advice about giving full feeds. So the first 4 weeks went pretty smoothly sleep-wise. But around 5 weeks our routine suddenly disintegrated. He would get sleepy on me, and I would put him down but he would cry and cry. So I'd get him up again. Sometimes he was then wide awake. Other times he was sleepy. Various people told me he was going through a growth spurt and his sleep patterns were changing. So I should just go with it for a few weeks and work on a routine later.

I did this, although it nearly killed me as during the waking hours he was very discontent. He hated lying under playgym, cried loudly in his bouncy chair, would only tolerate about 20 minutes in his pram before he had to be carried. So I basically ended up holding him all day. With hindsight I think this problem was equal parts of (a) not sleeping properly and so being cranky; (b) an inexperienced mother not letting him cry long enough sometimes (although I definitely tried at other times); and (c) his personality, which has always been very intense and alert and active.

He is now 10 months old and has not slept in his pushchair since he was 6 weeks old, for instance. (And he still lasts no longer than about 20 minutes.) Anyway at 8 weeks I decided I had to take control of this, as I was holding him every day from 6am to 11pm, when he would finally consent to be put down in his cot (asleep). I was exhausted and frustrated, and could not get out of the house and mix with people because of his high demands. It also made it difficult to eat properly and rest properly, let alone do any housework. This was probably the first big lowpoint after the birth.

I tried controlled crying on him and found I only ever got 2 results: (1) he would go to sleep from awake without a murmur; or (2) he would cry and cry for up to 1 hour 20 minutes before I gave in. He never actually cried himself to sleep. After 6 days of this, I saw only tiny improvements, and the constant crying was too stressful and guilt-inducing. I felt awful for putting him through it, and when he lost his voice from crying I just gave in. After that, I abandoned attempts to put him down awake as I had no confidence that he would fall asleep without hours of crying, and I felt too guilty about what I had put him through before.

Fortunately, right at that time (9 weeks old) someone recommended *The Contented Little Baby Book* to me. Within 48 hours of putting him on the routine, we had our evenings back. He settled well at 7pm, and finally my husband Rob and I could eat together, talk and have a little time to ourselves. It was golden!! While we tried to follow the routine as closely as we could, I had the consistent problem that he woke at 5am ready to start the day. This put the rest of the day's routine out of whack, so that I could never quite time things as suggested. I persevered as best I could and managed to maintain a 7pm bedtime, but his naps were usually at the wrong time, and he never slept as much as the book recommended.

At 4 months we travelled to relatives in Australia, and my highly sensitive alert baby was totally overwhelmed by the trip (only slept 2 out of 24 hours on the flight !!) and his sleep was totally erratic whilst there. The only way I could get him to sleep during the 3 weeks there was to have him in bed with me. Even then he woke frequently during the night and cried, and daytime naps were very difficult. Fortunately we had lots of grandparents, aunts etc. on hand to cuddle him while he slept, so we got through that time. By the time we got back, however, he had completely lost the ability to fall asleep by himself, and had all the wrong sleep associations.

The next month was the absolute worst since he was born. He was waking several times a night, and it got harder and harder to put him back to bed. At first a cuddle or a quick breastfeed would do it. But it took longer and longer to settle him back down. I would be leaning over the cot, lowering him inch by inch to the mattress, only to have him yell blue murder the second his back hit the mattress!

After a few weeks, he was waking 3–4 times between 7pm and 5.30am, and each time it was taking 45–50 minutes to settle him back down. So I was getting about 4 hours sleep a night broken into 40-minute bits. Needless to say, I was depressed, frustrated and exhausted and not enjoying motherhood at all.

At 5 months we did controlled crying with him. The first night it took 23 minutes. The next night 6 minutes and then 4 minutes and the problem was fixed. He slept from 7pm to 5am without waking at all. But at 5am he was up for the day. As before, I could never follow the routines exactly because of his early waking time. So I let him set his own naptimes, and he was having two naps, morning and afternoon, of 1–1½ hours each. Usually the afternoon nap was, say, 3–4pm, sometimes earlier, sometimes later.

However, one day when he was about 9 months I noticed that, by coincidence he went to sleep at his naptimes at about the time that the book said he should. And the next day he woke at 6.30am, which hadn't happened in AGES. So I kept an eye on him that day, and put him down for his naps according to the routine, even though he appeared not to be ready for the nap. To my surprise, he did go to sleep after 10 minutes or so of crying and slept well. And the next morning woke at 6.30am.

So I started wondering whether the daytime naps were the cause of his early morning waking.

After about a week of pushing him into the new pattern of daytime naps, I found that he was still waking at 5–5.30am, but unlike before he was not fully awake and ready to start the day. If I picked him up and cuddled him he would fall back asleep and he would sleep another 45 minutes or so.

Sometimes when he woke the second time, I could do it again. So although we were still getting disturbed, his wake-time had moved to 6–7am.

If things had continued this way, I don't think I would have bothered further. It would have been nice to stay in bed, but getting up for a quick cuddle and putting him back down was not so bad. THEN, as always with William, things got worse. I have basically found that no soft methods have ever worked with him. They might tide you over for a day or so, but pretty soon it won't work any more. It started taking longer and longer to put him back down. Then I couldn't get him back into his cot and had to hold him in my arms. (He wouldn't settle in bed with me, so I had to sit in the chair.) Then even that wouldn't work, and although he was tired he couldn't settle into a deep sleep.

As this morning sleep deteriorated, so did his lunch-time nap sleep. He has never slept as long as the routine suggests. A few weeks before he had been sleeping 30 minutes in the morning and 1½ hours or so at his lunch-time sleep. As time had gone on, this had gone down to 2 naps of 20 minutes, and sometimes only one. Needless to say, he was totally exhausted and grumpy. Clearly I had to act.

At this point I rang Gina, and we discussed what might be waking him: light, noise, hunger, dirty nappy, etc etc. He was regularly waking with a dirty nappy, so at Gina's suggestion I decreased the amount of fruit and vegetables he was having at tea-time and increased the amount of carbohydrate. He started waking clean 50 per cent of the time, but the waking continued. After eliminating any other cause, we decided that the only reason he was waking was because he couldn't settle himself back to sleep when he came into his light sleep around 5am. This also seemed to be the problem during the day – an inability to settle himself as he came into a light sleep.

So I decided to do controlled crying to fix the problem. I was pregnant and didn't relish early mornings with him after broken nights with Number Two, and I was very anxious to fix this problem while he was still young enough.

I was dreading it, as Gina told me that controlled crying for early morning waking could take two or three weeks, so I knew that we were really in for some trouble.

But I was absolutely determined, and in the end it only took one morning.

Gina and I decided that waking after 6am was acceptable long term, but before 6am was too early. I had also found that in the past few weeks that if he woke around 6.15am he could cope with the morning quite happily. Any earlier and he was tired and cranky. So we decided that if he woke after 6am I would get him up, but any time before that we would do controlled crying. The next morning he woke at 5.45am and cried for 2 hours. I went in and gave him a cup of milk around 6.30am, but left him to cry and he finally fell asleep at 7.45am. He woke after 20 minutes and went on with the day. (He was in a fantastic mood all day, I might add!) He slept 1 hour 20 minutes at lunch, and the next morning he woke at 6.30am.

And that was it. It is now 4 months since we did this sleep training. William has consistently slept until 6.45/7am ever since then. During this time he has cut 3 teeth and contracted conjunctivitis – but he is still sleeping beautifully! In addition, it appears his sleeping skills are getting even better, as his lunch time nap, which used to be a maximum of $1^{1}/_{2}$. hours has now extended to 2 hours and occasionally even $2^{1}/_{2}$. hours. He now sleeps better than any other baby I know, which amazes me when I consider how bad a sleeper he was for the first 6 months of his life.

I am a fairly laid-back person by nature, and never intended to have such a structured day for my son. But as the months have gone on, I have found that the more closely I stick to the routine, the happier he is – and the happier I am. Some babies can set their own routine and live happily with results. My baby cannot. Some babies show signs of tiredness when they are ready to sleep. Mine does not. (He just suddenly cracks when he is overtired and exhausted and then is incapable of relaxing into sleep.) Having such a routine to follow has saved all of us so much unhappiness. I hope this testimony is of some help to other parents who are struggling with the problem of early morning waking.

Postscript: I also passed on Gina's advice to a friend whose 11 month old was waking at 5am. It took her 3 days of controlled crying but since then she too has had no problem, and for the last month he has been waking around 7am each morning.

Your questions answered

Q **How many hours sleep a day does my newborn baby need?**

A • Depending on weight and whether the baby was premature most babies need approximately 16 hours a day, broken up into a series of short and long sleeps.

• Smaller babies and premature babies tend to need more sleep, and will be more likely to doze on and off between feeds.

• Larger babies are capable of staying awake for an hour or so and sleeping for at least one longer spell of four to five hours during a 24-hour period.

• By the age of one month, most babies who are feeding well and gaining weight (6–8oz a week) are capable of sleeping for one longer stretch of five to six hours between feeds.

Q **How do I make sure that the longer stretch of sleeping is always in the night and not during the day?**

A • Follow my routines and always start your day at 7am, so that you have enough time to fit in all the feeds before 11pm.

• Try to keep your baby awake for at least six to eight hours between 7am and 7pm.

• Ensure that your baby stays awake for as much of the two-hour social period as possible. Once he is awake a total of eight hours between 7am and 7pm, he will be more likely to sleep longer in the night.

• Always distinguish between sleep and awake time. During the first few weeks put the baby in a dark room for all sleeps.

• Do not talk to your baby or overstimulate him during the feeds between 7pm and 7am.

Q I am trying to stick to your routines but my four-week-old baby can only stay awake for an hour at the most after feeds. Should I be trying to make him stay awake longer?

A • If your baby is feeding well and gaining between 6–8oz per week, sleeping well between feeds in the night, and alert for some of his awake periods during the day, he is just one of those babies who needs more sleep.

• If he is waking up more than twice in the night or staying awake for over an hour in the night despite feeding well at 11pm, try stimulating him a bit more during the day.

• While the 11pm feed should always be a quiet feed, a baby under three months needs to be awake for 45 minutes. A sleepy feed at this time will most certainly result in a baby being more awake around 2–3am.

• If you structure your baby's feeds and sleep times between 7am and 11pm by my routines, when your baby does cut back his sleep, it will be at the right time.

Q The routine seems very restricting. If I go out with my four-week-old during waking time he goes straight to sleep in the buggy, which means he has slept too much.

A • Whether your baby is in my routine or not, during the first couple of months life is restrictive due to the amount of time spent feeding.

• By two months most babies are capable of going longer between feeds and are quicker at feeding. This makes outings easier.

• For the first two months if you plan your outings to fit around his sleep time, by eight weeks he will be able to stay awake longer when you take him out in the car or buggy.

Q My four-week-old baby has suddenly started to wake up at nine in the evening. If I feed him then he wakes up twice in the night at 1am and 5am. I have tried making him hold out until 10pm, but then he is so tired he doesn't feed properly, which means he still wakes up earlier.

A • Around one month the light and deep sleep become much more defined. I find that a lot of babies come into a very light sleep around 9pm, so ensure that the area around the nursery is not subject to loud, sudden noises and that the baby cannot hear your voice at this time.

- Breast-fed babies may need a top-up of expressed milk after the 6pm feed.
- If you have to feed him at 9pm try to settle him with one breast or a couple of ounces, then push the 10.30pm feed to 11.30pm. Hopefully he will then take a full feed, which would get him through to 3.30am.

Q I always have to wake my baby of ten weeks for his 10.30pm feed, then he only takes 90–120ml (3–4oz) and wakes again at 4am. Could I just drop the last feed and see if he goes through until 4am without that feed?

A • I would not advise getting rid of the feed yet, as he could wake up at 1am and then 5am, which in effect would be two night wakings. I have always found it best to get the baby sleeping through to 7am, and taking solids, before dropping the 11pm feed. This usually happens between three and four months.

- Make sure he is tucked in properly; often a baby getting out of his blankets and thrashing around in his light sleep is enough to arouse him to a fully awake state. If he is not getting out of his covers, I would wait 10–15 minutes before going to him, then I would try settling him with some water. If he settles with the water he will make up for the lost feed during the day, and at his age the increased daily milk intake usually has the knock-on effect of him not needing to feed in the night. If he does not settle with the water I would try to settle him with a small feed and try again in a couple of weeks.
- If, by the time he reaches four months, he has started solids, but is still waking up, I would be inclined to offer him water for a few nights, then get tough if that did not work. This of course could only be done if your baby was gaining the right amount of weight each week and getting the right amount of milk and food during the day.

Q My friend's baby of three months does not have a set sleep plan during the day, yet he sleeps well at night and seems very happy. Does it really matter about establishing day-time sleep?

A • Recent research shows that children up to the age of two years benefit physically and psychologically from a proper structured nap in the middle of the day.

• During the first few months many babies are happy to doze on and off in a car seat or Moses basket, which can be very convenient for the parents as it allows them more flexibility. Unfortunately once the baby becomes bigger and more active he is unlikely to fall alseep happily in the car seat. It can then be very difficult to get him to sleep in his big cot during the day.

• Sleep in a car seat is usually short and of poor quality; as he gets older he will most likely spend most of his day catnapping and become overtired and irritable.

Q My six-month-old baby, who has always slept 45 minutes in the morning, plus a good two hours at lunch time, now wakes up after one hour and refuses to go back to sleep no matter how long I leave her. She also refuses to take a nap later in the afternoon, which means she is very grumpy for most of the afternoon and needs to go to bed at 6pm. This is starting to result in earlier and earlier waking times.

A • Check she is not being disturbed by older children playing near by or by the vacuum cleaner. Make sure that the room is really dark, and that she is tucked in really well.

• Ensure that she is getting enough physical exercise in the morning; at this age she should spend a great deal of her waking time on the floor, rolling and kicking.

• Make sure that she is not going to sleep before 9am, and cut back this nap by ten minutes every three days until she ends up with a nap of no more than 20–25 minutes in the morning.

Q At what age do you think a baby can go without a day-time nap?

A • In my experience all babies and young children benefit from properly structured sleep until they are at least two years of age. As they get older they may not need to sleep during the day, but a period of quiet time in their bed is always beneficial to both toddler and mother.

• Most very young babies need three naps a day. The naps should be made up of one long nap and two shorter naps. Between four and six months the baby normally cuts back on the late afternoon nap until he manages to get through to bedtime without it.

• Between the age of 15 months and 18 months your baby will show signs of wanting to drop his second nap. You should always encourage it to be the morning nap.

• If he drops the afternoon nap and has a two-hour nap in the morning, he will be exhausted by 6pm and go into a very deep sleep at 7pm. This usually has the knock-on effect of an earlier wake-up time in the morning.

Q Why do you keep stressing the importance of allowing the baby to wake up naturally? My husband thinks it is cruel to leave our 8-week-old son lying in his cot alone and that he should be picked up the minute he wakes.

A • In the very early days the majority of babies will cry for food the minute they wake. As they get bigger and older and able to go longer spells between feeds the cry for food immediately on waking decreases. By allowing your baby this short spell of gradual waking you will be able to tell if your baby is really hungry or ready to go longer between feeds. All babies come into a light sleep between 5am and 6am in the morning. I have found that by encouraging them to lie in their cots for short spells on waking from their daytime naps, they are much more likely to go back to sleep when they wake at 5am or 6am.

Q Can you describe what you mean by settling the baby, as you say that the baby should not be cuddled prior to sleep times.

A • By all means cuddle your baby prior to sleep times, but try not to cuddle him to sleep as he may learn the wrong sleep associations and become dependent on a cuddle to get off to sleep. In the early days when he is feeding little and often this may not appear to be a problem. But as he gets older and his sleep cycles change and he no longer needs a feed in the night, you may find that you are still getting up to him several times a night when he comes into his light sleep as he is unable to get back to sleep without a cuddle.

 • In the very first few weeks I always try to get my babies to their room at least ten minutes before they get sleepy so that we can have a short wind-down time and a cuddle. While I do cuddle them I do not talk to them or have eye contact as I believe that it could send confusing signals. This can lead to some babies finding it more difficult to settle. It is also very important that you try to settle your baby in the cot when he is getting sleepy but not fully asleep. Not all babies will drift off to sleep naturally and some may have to learn to get off to sleep by themselves. Provided your baby is really ready to sleep and has been well fed and winded, it is advisable to allow him a short crying-down period. Parents who allow their baby to learn how to settle himself in the very early days will rarely have to go through the procedure of sleep training their baby at a later stage because he has learned all the wrong sleep associations.

Q I have been following your routines since birth with my six-week-old baby but find that she can only stay awake for one and half hours at a time not the two hours that you advise during the day. I am sure that this is probably the reason that she is still waking at 2am, which can often mean a second waking between 5am and 6am.

A • Your baby will eventually start to stay awake longer during the day but until this happens, I would suggest that you have her awake slightly longer than the rec-ommended one hour at her last feed. I would advise that you start to wake her up no later than 9.45pm so she is wide awake at 10pm.

- Give her the first breast or two-thirds of her formula feed and then keep her wide awake until 11.15pm, at which time she should have her nappy changed, then the lights dimmed before being offered the second breast or a further couple of ounces of freshly made formula. By splitting the feed and having the baby awake slightly longer at this time, I usually find that they stretch a further hour or two in the night and by getting past 3am find that I am only getting up once in the night.

- Once the baby sleeps through regularly to 7am, then you can gradually cut back on the time she is awake at 10pm by five minutes every three or four nights. Finally, while it is important to have her wide awake at 10pm, do not mentally stimulate her too much.

Q My baby is nine weeks old and was sleeping until nearly 6am for almost two weeks, but since moving him onto the eight to twelve week routine, he has started to wake earlier and earlier.

A • I would suggest that you re-introduce the 5pm feed. It is more than likely that your baby has cut back hard on the 10pm feed since he has been taking more at 6.15pm. By going back to a split feed at 5pm and 6.15pm your baby should take more at the 10pm feed, which he obvi-ously still needs.

- Once he has been sleeping through regularly to nearly 7am for a couple of weeks, you can try gradually reduc-ing the 5pm feed and eventually dropping it when your son shows signs that he is capable of getting through the night on a smaller late feed.

Q My eight-week-old baby has followed your routines to the letter, but for the last week he has started to wake up after 30-45 minutes of going down for his midday nap. He will only settle back to sleep if I feed him. This is having the knock-on effect that he refuses to feed at 2.30pm, often not taking anything until 3.30pm, resulting in a poor feed at 6.15pm and now he has started waking earlier for his late feed.

A • It is around this age that a baby takes on an adult sleep cycle pattern and it poses a very common problem. The majority of babies who have learnt the right sleep associations will, if allowed, settle themselves back to sleep within 5–10 minutes of coming into their light sleep, but some babies will awaken fully and actually fuss for a good 10–20 minutes before going back to sleep. In my experience, parents who are not prepared to allow their babies to settle themselves back to sleep at this nap usually end up with a baby who is irritable and grumpy all afternoon through the lack of sleep. Although it is very difficult to leave a young baby of this age to cry himself back to sleep, within a few days the baby normally has learned how to settle himself back to sleep and long-term problems can be avoided. If a baby does seem genuinely hungry after the 45 minutes I would suggest that he is given a top-up prior to him going down for his nap. This way you can be reassured that when the baby comes into his light sleep that it is not hunger that is preventing him from returning to sleep.

• Once the baby has been sleeping through the lunch-time nap for a couple of weeks, gradually reduce the amount he is being topped up until you feel confident about cutting it altogether.

Q Our four-month-old baby has been demand fed since birth and will only sleep in our arms, her car seat or with us in our bed. Last week we started to put her into your routines; the feeding routine is going well, but when we try to settle her in her cot in the nursery she becomes hysterical.

A • I would advise you to keep sticking to the times for her
feeding and sleeping, but until she gets used to her big
cot and nursery continue to get her to sleep the way
you have been doing in the past. However, do make
sure that the times she does sleep are at the times on the
routine, as this will make the eventual transfer to her
cot and nursery easier.

• Get her used to her nursery gradually by taking her in
there in her car seat for short spells several times a day.
Put the car seat with her in it into the cot and sit close
by her playing with toys and talking to her. Start off by
doing this for five minutes at a time – building up to ten
minutes. Once she shows signs of being happy there,
gradually move the chair further and further from the
cot; keep talking to her and reassuring her the whole
time. When you reach the stage when she is happy for
you to potter around the room while she sits there, you
can advance to lying her down in the cot and repeat the
whole procedure again.

• Once she is happy to lie in her cot for 15–20 minutes
you should get her used to you going out of the room
for short spells. Start off by leaving the room for a
minute at a time every five minutes. By gradually building up the time you are out of the room you should
reach a stage where she is happy to lie for 15–20
minutes or so under her mobile and looking at her toys.
When this happens you should be able to start to settle
her there for her naps without too much fuss. She may
cry for a short spell when put down, but it will not be
as traumatic as just putting her down and leaving her to
cry all alone in a strange room.

• This problem could easily be avoided if babies were
introduced to their nursery and big cot from the very
beginning. Even if you plan to have the baby in with
you for the first few months, you should do some feeds
in the nursery, change nappies there and get the baby
used to lying in his big cot for short spells when he is

awake. A good time for this is when you are preparing the bath. Propping some colourful books around the sides of the cot will normally capture the interest of most babies for short spells.

Q We are planning to visit family in the USA for three weeks when the baby is seven months old. She has slept through the night since she was nine weeks and is a near perfect 'contented baby'. Have you any suggestions that would help us keep her in the routine once we are over there?

A • I have travelled all over the world with my babies and had very few problems keeping them in the routine. I believe that this is because I put them straight into the routine in the local time the following day after we arrive, regardless of how often or how early they awoke the first night in our new destination.

• On the first day of arrival you may have to adjust the routine. For example; if she has slept a lot on the plane it would be pointless to try and settle her at 7pm local time. Instead, let her have short nap early evening, then follow the 5pm to 7pm at a later time, like 9pm to 11pm. Then the following day, start her routine as normal – local time.

• In my experience parents who allow their babies to get over-stimulated and over-handled on holiday are far more likely to have disrupted nights. Therefore, try to keep the bed and bath time routine the same as at home. Do not allow her to get too excited or over-handled by well meaning relations prior to the bath, and no visitors in her bedroom at put down.

• If she wakes in the night or wakes earlier, settle her with a cuddle or water for a couple of nights.

• Aim to keep her daytime routine on track and after a couple of nights, if she still wakes, try leaving her for 10–20 minutes before rushing to her. Parents who follow these guidelines usually tell me that within three to four days the baby is back on track and settling into the routine on local time.

Q I am following your routines with my four-week-old baby
and everything is going well, but I am concerned that my
life is going to be very restricted when the time comes for
me to take her to play groups, swimming and other social
activities. So many of these activities take place around the
lunchtime nap. Does this mean that the routine will go all
wrong if I try to adjust her sleep on those days we want to
participate in outside activities?

A • Because it will be another four weeks at least before you
start to take your baby swimming etc, I am fairly confident that you should be able to alter the routines a couple
of days a week to fit in with these social activities.

• The key to altering the routines is to try and avoid altering them two days in a row. In my experience a baby
under four months who has his routine altered two or
three days on the run is more likely to suffer from a
build up of over-tiredness. An over-tired baby will
become very irritable and very hard to settle, which
usually leads to more middle-of-the-night wakings.

• In the early days of building up your baby's social life,
try to avoid altering his routine more than twice a week.
Once he can cope with these changes you could build up
to three changes a week.

• The important thing to remember when altering the
routines is that a baby under four months can rarely
stay awake longer than two hours at a time before
becoming over-tired.

• When altering the routines it is important to structure
them according to how long your baby can happily stay
awake before becoming over-tired. If she has to have a
shorter morning nap she may need to go down much
earlier for the lunchtime nap. If you have to cut her
lunchtime nap short, then you may have to give her extra
sleep late afternoon so she isn't over-tired at bedtime.

• However you change her daytime sleep, try to ensure
that the overall total does not exceed the recommended
daily total for her age.

Common problems in the first few months | 5

Burping

It is important to follow your baby's lead regarding when to stop and wind him. If you constantly interrupt his feed to try and get his wind up, he will be likely to get so upset and frustrated that the crying will cause more wind than the feed itself. Time and time again I watch babies being thumped endlessly on the back, the mother refusing to continue with the feed as she is convinced the baby has wind. The reality is that very few babies need to be burped more than once during a feed and once at the end.

A breast-feeding baby will pull himself off the breast when he is ready to burp. If he has not done so by the end of the first breast, you can try burping before putting him on the second breast. Bottle-fed babies will normally drink half to three-quarters of their feed and pull themselves off to be burped. Regardless of whether you are breast feeding or bottle feeding, if you adopt the correct holding position as illustrated on pages 44 and 67, your baby should bring his wind up quickly and easily both during and at the end of the feed. If your baby does not bring up the wind within a few minutes it is best to leave it and try later. More often than not he will bring it up after he has been laid flat for his nappy change.

Occasionally a baby passing excessive wind from his rear end can suffer considerable discomfort and become very distressed. A breast-feeding mother should keep a close eye on her diet to see if a particular food or drink is causing the wind. Citrus fruits or drinks taken in excess can sometimes cause severe wind in some babies. The other culprits are chocolate and excessive dairy intake.

Special care should be taken to make sure that the baby is reaching the hind milk. Too much fore milk can cause explosive bowel movements and excessive passing of wind.

With a bottle-fed baby who is already feeding from the special anti-colic bottles, the cause of the excessive wind is usually overfeeding. If your baby is regularly drinking 90–180ml (3–6oz) a day more than the amount advised on the packet, and constantly putting on in excess of 8oz of weight each week, cut back on a couple of his feeds (either the 2.30pm or the 5pm) for a few days to see if there is any improvement. A 'sucky' baby could be offered a dummy after the smaller feeds to satisfy his sucking needs.

The correct burping position

Sometimes a teat with a hole either too small or too large for your baby's needs could cause excessive wind. Experiment with the different sizes of teats; sometimes using a smaller hole at a couple of the feeds can help a baby who is drinking some of his feeds too quickly.

Colic

Colic is a common problem for babies under three months. It can make life miserable for the baby and the parents, and to date there is no cure for it. There are over-the-counter medications, but most parents with a baby suffering from severe colic say they are of little help. Although a baby can suffer from colic at any time of the day, the most common time seems to be between 6pm and midnight. Parents resort to endless feeding, rocking, patting, driving the baby round the block, most of which seem to bring little or no relief. Colic usually disappears by four months of age, but by that time the baby has usually learnt all the wrong sleep associations, so the parents are no further forward.

Parents who contact me for help with their 'colicky baby' describe how the baby screams, often for hours at a time, thrashes madly and keeps bringing up his legs in pain. These babies all seem to have one thing in common: they are all being fed on demand. Feeding this way all too often leads to the baby having another feed before the first one has been digested, one of the reasons that I believe may cause colic. (See also the advice on Feeding bottles on pages 19–20.)

Not one of the babies I have cared for has ever suffered from colic and I am convinced that it is because I structure their feeding and sleeping from day one. When I do go in to help an older baby who is suffering from colic it seems to disappear within 24 hours of them being put on to the routine.

Firstly, I would check that the colic is being caused by demand feeding and not the mother's diet. Then depending on the age, the symptoms of the baby, and how often they were feeding throughout the evening and the middle of the night, I would introduce sugar water. With a baby between one and three months of age who is feeding excessively in the night and consistently putting on more than the recommended weight gain each week, I would try to replace one of the night feeds with some sugar water. When the baby wakes in the night I would give 120ml (4oz) of cool boiled water mixed with half a teaspoon of sugar to settle him. At this stage I find plain boiled water does not have the same effect. The following day I would wake the baby at 7am, regardless of how little sleep he has had in the night, and then proceed with the routine throughout the day to 6.30pm. At this time I would always offer a breast-fed baby a top-up of expressed milk to ensure that he has had enough to drink. This avoids him needing to feed again in two hours, which is a common pattern in babies suffering from colic. With a bottle-fed baby I always make sure that the 2.30pm feed is smaller so that he feeds well at 6.30pm.

With an older baby of three months or more I would attempt to eliminate middle of the night feeds altogether or at least reduce them to only one. In both cases it is important to ensure that the baby feeds well at 6.15pm, if necessary offering a top up of expressed milk at this time. A low milk supply early evening is often the cause of a baby feeding little and often which can lead to them not digesting feeds properly.

More often than not the baby settles well the first night, but occasionally I may get a baby who has developed the wrong sleep associations, as a result of the colic. With these babies I use the controlled crying method of sleep training and within three to four nights they are going down happily and sleeping well until the 10.30pm feed. Because they have slept well and have gone a full four hours since their last feed, they feed well and will go on to last for an even longer spell in the night. Depending on their age they are given either a feed or sugar water. A baby of three months or older who is capable of going from the last feed through to 6am or 7am should be given sugar water for a week. Once the pattern of once-a-night waking is established, gradually reduce the amount of sugar until he is taking plain water.

This method, along with the routines, will encourage a baby who has suffered from colic and developed the wrong sleep assocations to sleep through the night, normally within a couple of weeks. I cannot stress strongly enough that the success of this method very much depends on the use of the sugar water during the first week. Plain water does not have the same success. I am not sure why the sugar water method works; it is a tip I picked up from an older maternity nurse over 25 years ago and it has never failed me. Parents are often concerned that it will encourage their babies to develop a sweet tooth, or even worse rot their teeth. Because of the short period of time the sugar water is used I have never seen any of these problems occur. I am also pleased to say that my advice has now been backed up by recent research on colic by Dr Peter Lewindon of the Royal Children's Hospital, Brisbane, Australia. Research shows that sugar stimulates the body's natural painkillers and that some babies suffering from colic can be helped by the sugar water solution.

Crying

Obviously all new parents are anxious to make their newborn baby's introduction to the world a happy one. As we all associate crying with pain or unhappiness I can understand why, as a new parent, you will be prepared to do virtually anything to stop your baby crying. A newborn baby's only way of communicating is by crying, and it is important that you do not fall into the trap of thinking the only way of dealing with crying is by feeding your baby.

Listed below are the main reasons a healthy baby would cry. Use it as a check list to eliminate the possible causes for your baby crying, so you can satisfy his real needs.

Hunger

This is most likely to happen in the evening if you have not established a good milk supply. Try resting in the afternoon for a short spell to help increase your milk for the evening feed. Try offering your baby a top-up of expressed milk until you increase your milk supply.

Tiredness

Babies under six weeks tend to get tired after one hour of being awake. Although they may not be quite ready to sleep, they need to be kept quiet and calm.

Overtiredness

No baby under three months should be allowed to stay awake for more than two hours at a time, as they can become very overtired and impossible to settle. If your baby is fretful two hours after his feed or from the time he wakes up, he should be calmed down and encouraged to sleep, even if he does not look tired. Care should also be taken not to over-stimulate the baby 30 minutes prior to being put to bed. Overtiredness is one of the main reasons young babies do not sleep well.

Boredom

Even a newborn baby needs to be awake some of the time. Encourage him to be awake for a short spell after his day feeds. Babies under one month love to look at anything black and white, especially pictures of faces.

Wind

All babies take a certain amount of wind while feeding, bottle-fed babies more so than breast-fed ones. Given the opportunity, most babies bring up their wind easily. If you suspect that your baby's crying is caused by wind, check that you are allowing enough time between feeds. I have found overfeeding and demand feeding to be the main causes of colic in young babies. A breast-fed baby needs at least three hours to digest a full feed, and a formula-fed baby should be allowed three and a half to four hours.

I have read in many leading baby books that most young babies cry on average a total of two hours in a day. This is also the information given by the Thomas Coram Research Unit at London University. They also claim that at six weeks crying reaches a peak, with 25 per cent of babies crying and fussing for at least four hours a day. Dr St James-Roberts also claims that 40 per cent of the crying occurs between 6pm and midnight. Dutch researchers Hetty Van de Rijt and Frank Plooij, authors of *Why They Cry* (HarperCollins), have spent over 20 years studying baby development and they claim that babies become troublesome and demanding when they are going through one of the seven major neurological changes that occur during the first year.

With very young babies I have noticed that they do go through a more unsettled stage around three weeks and six weeks, which tends to coincide with growth spurts. However, I would be absolutely horrified if any of my babies cried for even one hour a day, let alone two to four hours! The one thing that parents comment upon time and time again is how happy their baby is on the routine. Of course my babies do cry; some may cry when they have their nappy changed, others cry when having their faces washed and a few try to fight sleep when put in their cots. With the ones that fight sleep, because I know they are well fed, burped and ready to sleep I am very strict. I would let them fuss and yell for 10–20 minutes until they have settled themselves. This is the only real crying I experience, and even then it is with the minority of my babies and lasts for no longer than a week or two. Understandably all parents hate to hear their baby cry; many are worried that to put their baby down in a cot to sleep and leave him to cry like this, could be psychologically damaging. I would like to reassure you that provided your baby has been well fed, and that you have followed the routines regarding awake periods and wind-down time, your baby will not suffer psychological damage. In the long term you will have a happy, contented baby who has learned to settle himself to sleep. Many parents who have followed the demand method with the first baby, and my routines with their second baby, would confirm wholeheartedly that my methods are by far the best and, in the long term, the easiest.

Marc Weissbluth MD, Director of the The Sleep Disorders Center at the Children's Memorial Hospital, Chicago, says in his book *Healthy Sleep Habits, Happy Child* (Vermilion) that parents should remember they are allowing their baby to cry, not making him cry. He also says that it is much harder for an older baby to learn how to settle himself if he's not been allowed to cry. Therefore, do not feel guilty or cruel if you have to allow a short spell of crying when your baby is going off to sleep. He will very quickly learn to settle himself, as long as you have made sure he is well fed, and has been awake enough, but not so long that he is overtired.

Dummies

The majority of babycare experts frown upon the use of a dummy, claiming that a sucky baby should be allowed to find his thumb. While the majority of very young babies are able to find their thumb, I have yet to see one who can keep it in his mouth long enough to achieve any sucking pleasure. In reality, it takes nearly three months for a baby to develop enough co-ordination to keep his thumb in his mouth for any length of time.

I am amazed how some parents prefer to stick their own fingers in their baby's mouth and spend hour after hour rocking and walking the floor with their baby rather than give him a dummy. They choose to end up with a very demanding baby who refuses to be put down or even to sit for 15 minutes in a baby chair, just because they do not want to give him a dummy.

If used with discretion I think a dummy can be a great asset, especially for a sucky baby. However, I must stress the importance of never allowing your baby to have the dummy in his cot or allowing him to suck himself to sleep on the dummy. By all means use it to calm him and if necessary to settle him at sleep times, **but remove it before he falls asleep**. He may yell for a short time but he will soon learn not to expect it while sleeping. Allowing a baby to fall asleep with a dummy in his mouth is one of the worst sleep association problems to try and solve. He can end up waking several times a night, and each time he will expect the dummy to get back to sleep. This problem can easily be avoided if the dummy is removed just before he drops off to sleep.

I have used dummies with a great number of my babies and have not encountered any serious problems. By being selective in their use I find that by the age of three months the majority of my babies are rejecting them. If a baby reaches four months and is still using the dummy, I would gradually wean him from using it over a period of two weeks; any longer could lead to real attachment problems.

There are two types of dummy available. One has a round cherry-type teat, the other has a flat-shaped teat, which is called an orthodontic teat. Some experts claim that the orthodontic teat shape is better for the baby's mouth, but the problem with this type is that most young babies cannot hold them in for very long. I tend to use the cherry-type teat, and so far none of my babies appear to have developed an overbite, which is often the result of a dummy being used excessively once the teeth have come through. Whichever type of dummy you choose, buy several, thus allowing them to be changed frequently. The utmost attention should be paid to cleanliness when using a dummy; it should be washed and sterilized after each use. Never clean it by licking it as one sees so many parents do; there are more germs and bacteria in the mouth than you could believe.

Hiccups

Hiccups are very normal among tiny babies, and very few get distressed by them. Hiccups often happen after a feed. If it has been a night-time feed and your baby is due to go down for a sleep, it is advisable to go ahead and put him down regardless. If you wait until the hiccups have finished there is a bigger chance of him falling asleep in your arms, which is something to be avoided at all costs. If your baby is one of the rare ones who gets upset by his hiccups, give him the recommended dose of gripe water.

Possetting

It is very common for some babies to bring up a small amount of milk while being burped or after a feed. It is called possetting, and for most babies it does not create a problem. However, if your baby is regularly gaining more than 8oz of weight each week it could be that he is drinking too much. With a bottle-fed baby the problem is easily solved as you are able to see how much the baby is drinking and therefore slightly reduce the amount at the feeds during which he appears to possett more. It is more difficult to tell how much a breast-fed baby is drinking. But by keeping a note of which feeds cause more possetting, and reducing the time on the breast at those feeds, the possetting may be reduced.

If your baby is possetting excessively and not gaining weight it could be that he is suffering from a condition called 'reflux'. If your baby does have reflux, your doctor can prescribe a medication to be given either before or with a feed, which helps keep the milk down. With babies who are inclined to bring up milk, it is important to keep them as upright as possible after a feed, and special care should be taken when burping.

Any baby bringing up an entire feed twice in a row should be seen by a doctor immediately.

Reflux

Sometimes a baby displaying all the symptoms of colic actually has a condition called gastro-oesophageal reflux. Because the muscle at the lower end of the oesophagus is too weak to keep the milk in the baby's stomach, it comes back up, along with acid from the stomach, causing a very painful burning sensation in the oesophagus. Excessive possetting is one of the symptoms of reflux. However, not all babies with reflux actually sick up the milk, and these babies can often be mis-diagnosed as having colic. They are often very difficult to feed, constantly arching their backs and screaming during a feed. They also tend to get very irritable when laid flat and no amount of cuddling or rocking will calm them when they are like this. If your baby displays these symptoms, insist that your doctor does a reflux test. I have seen too many cases of babies being diagnosed as having colic, when in fact they were suffering from reflux, despite not being sick. It is important that a baby with reflux is not overfed and is kept as upright as possible during and after feeding. Some babies may need medication for several months until the muscles tighten up. Fortunately the majority of babies outgrow the condition by the time they reach one year old.

Alice: aged six weeks

Alice was four weeks old when I went to help care for her. I had helped look after her elder brother Patrick, then aged two, for six weeks when he was born. He had been a model baby and had gone into the routine from day one. He slept through the night at six weeks and had continued to do so ever since; he had always been a good feeder and a very easy baby. I felt confident that the mother would only need me for four weeks with the second baby, as she had always shown an excellent understanding of sleep rhythms, the importance of the right sleep associations and the correct structuring of feeds.

It therefore came as a bit of a shock to find that Alice was not quite in 'the routine'. Her sleeping pattern was fine: she settled well at 7pm, I woke her at 10pm, she fed well and would sleep until 5am and her lunch-time sleep was also good. The problem was that she would not be put down to sleep during the day. I was rather surprised to find her mother carrying her everywhere, as she had been insistent when Patrick was a baby that he should learn to sit happily in his chair or go on his play mat for short spells. After several days of helping care for Alice I could see why she had to be held the whole time as the minute she was put on the floor or in her bouncy chair, she went berserk. In the long term, when the mother was going to have to care for both children, we could see that this was going to be a problem. Alice's six-week check with the doctor only confirmed what we already knew, that for her age she was very advanced, both mentally and physically. However, he could offer no real advice on how to make life happier for her and for the rest of us during the day.

In desperation we were referred to a paediatrician. I suggested that although Alice never brought up any milk, she did show some behaviour signs of 'reflux'. He was adamant that she did not have reflux and suggested that perhaps we were spoiling her and that we should be stricter about leaving her in her chair. Over the two weeks that followed, despite very small last feeds at 7pm and 10pm, Alice would sleep well at night. However, the days got worse and she screamed and screamed and screamed. Things came to a head when she started to scream and arch her back the minute we tried to feed her. We went to see the paediatrician for the second time, as I was convinced she did have reflux, but he was just as adamant as the previous time, and because she was never sick said it could not be reflux. A further two weeks went past with Alice's behaviour getting worse and worse. A third visit was booked to the paediatrician. This time the mother was insistent that the test be done and agreed to pay for it herself. The result came back positive: Alice had very serious reflux. She was given medication and her behaviour immediately began to improve; she would spend time on her play mat happily looking at her toys and the feeding got easier.

The sad thing about Alice is that as a very small baby she must have suffered a lot of pain. All too often babies are dismissed as being difficult or having colic, when in fact they are suffering from reflux, which is a problem that a great many doctors seem keen not to acknowledge.

Sleepy feeder

Sometimes a very sleepy baby may be inclined to keep dozing during the feed, but if he does not take the required amount he will end up wanting to feed again in an hour or two. This is a good time to change his nappy and burp him and encourage him to finish his feed. Making a little effort in the early days to keep your baby awake enough to drink the correct amount at each feed, and at the times given on the routine, will in the long term be well worthwhile. Some babies will take half the feed, have a stretch and kick for 10–15 minutes and then be happy to take the rest. During the first month allow up to 45 minutes for a feed.

Establishing a routine | 6

What makes a good routine?

Most young babies can stay awake for up to two hours. If your baby stays awake for longer than two hours he will generally become so exhausted that he will need a much longer sleep at his next nap time. This will have a knock-on effect: altering the rest of his routine, resulting in poor evening and night-time sleep. Therefore it is essential that you structure the two-hourly awake period properly, so that the feeding and sleeping plan works well.

Babies learn by association. It is very important that from day one he learns the right associations, and to differentiate between feeding, playing, cuddling and sleeping.

Feeding

Small babies spend a great deal of their waking time feeding. In order to avoid excessive night feeding, it is important to structure and establish a good daytime feeding pattern.

A breast-fed baby needs at least three hours to digest a full feed, and a bottle-fed baby needs three and a half to four hours. If you feed him before he really needs it, it is very likely that he will only take an ounce or two and will need feeding again in a couple of hours. This can lead to demand feeding, which is more likely to cause a build-up of wind in his digestive tract. Do not let him cry excessively before a feed as this can also cause wind. Do not overstimulate or distract him while feeding as he will lose interest after a couple of ounces. Avoid talking on the telephone for long periods while feeding. It is important that you concentrate and ensure that your baby feeds well. He should always be fed in a position where his back is straight. Do not rock him, as he will think it is sleep time, and if he is sleepy while feeding he will be more likely to vomit.

Playing

All babies love to be cuddled, talked and sung to. Research also shows that even very small babies like to look at simple books and interesting toys. For your baby to enjoy these things it is important that you do them at the right time. The best time is usually approximately one hour after he is awake and not hungry. He should never be played with or over-stimulated 20 minutes prior to his nap.

Because babies learn by association, I find that dividing toys and books into wake-up and wind-down toys a great help. Musical cot mobiles and colourful baby gyms, plus black and white cot cloth books are all excellent for keeping young babies interested for short spells, as are postcards and posters that show single objects or faces. Using these toys only at social times and having two or three different less stimulating toys for wind-down times can help. Babies have very short concentration spans; constantly talking and handling a baby during the social time can often result in the baby becoming overstimulated. It's important to take the cue from your baby as to how much stimulation he can handle. Even from a very young age babies should be encouraged to occupy themselves for short periods. This is much more likely to happen if the baby is left lying alone on a playmat or under his cot mobile, as he will be much more likely to kick and move around than when he is being held.

Cuddling

Babies need lots of cuddling, but it should always be done when your baby needs it, not when *you* need it. A baby needs energy to grow so it is important that you do not over-handle his small body and exhaust him. While all babies need to be nurtured, they are not toys; satisfy his needs, not your own. Differentiate the type of cuddle during his play time from that of wind-down time. Wind-down cuddling should have no eye contact, just closeness of bodies. It is important that your baby is not cuddled to sleep while feeding. After one hour of being awake and fed he should be happy to spend a little time amusing himself; if you constantly cuddle him during play time he will be less likely to respond to the cuddles that would normally help settle him for his nap. When cuddling him during the wind-down time, do not talk and avoid eye contact, as it can overstimulate him and result in him becoming overtired and not settling.

Sleep

It is essential for your baby's mental and physical development that he gets enough sleep; without the right amount of sleep your baby will become irritable, fretful and inconsolable.

Along with the routines, the following hints will help your baby develop healthy sleeping habits.

- Try to keep him awake for a short spell after his day feeds.
- Do not let him sleep too long in the late afternoon.
- Follow the same routine every evening; do not allow visitors in the nursery during wind-down time.
- Do not let him get overtired; allow at least one hour for the bath, feed and wind-down time.
- Do not overstimulate him or play with him after his bath.
- Do not rock him to sleep in your arms; try to settle him in his cot before he goes into a deep sleep.
- If you use a dummy to wind him down, remove it before you put him in his cot.
- If he falls asleep on the breast or bottle, rouse him slightly before settling him in his cot.

Structuring milk feeds during the first year

During the first few weeks, regardless of whether babies are breast or formula fed, not all can manage a strict four-hourly feeding pattern. By two weeks, if your baby has regained his birth weight and weighs over 7lb, he should manage to last three to four hours between feeds, provided he is getting a full feed at the times stated in the routines. By structuring feeds in the early days you can achieve several slots of three-hour feeding and some of four hours. If you structure his feeds according to the routines, the four-hour stretch between feeds should always happen between 10am and 2pm and 7pm to 7am. This would mean that a baby who fed at 6pm should get to 10pm, then feed again around 2/3am, then get to 6/7am.

Remember that the three-hour stretch between feeds is timed from the beginning of one feed to the beginning of the next; a baby starting to feed at 7am would then need to start his next feed at 10am. However, if you feel your baby is genuinely hungry before his next feed is due it is common sense to feed him, but also advisable to get to the root of the problem as to why he is not taking a full feed at the times stated on the routines. If you are breastfeeding it may be that he needs longer on the second breast; if you are bottle feeding it may be that he needs an extra ounce at some feeds.

Between the second and fourth week, most babies who are gaining 6–8oz each week are able to last slightly longer after one feed – usually four and a half to five hours. If you structure your baby's feeds, this will automatically be at the right time, ie between 11pm and 7am.

If your baby has been demand fed and you are attempting to put him into a routine, I would advise that you go back through the routines and put him into a routine that seems nearest to his demand-fed pattern. For example, a nine-week-old baby may need to start on the two to four week schedule. Once he is happy in that routine you should be able to work your way through the next two sets of routines within seven to 10 days. By the time he reaches 12 weeks he should be happily feeding at the times stated in the routine for his age. However, although it may take slightly longer for him to sleep through the night, the important thing is that he is only feeding once in the night and gradually increases the length of time he sleeps from his last feed, over a period of several weeks. Once the baby starts to sleep longer in the night it is important to keep a close eye on how you structure feeds, as things can go wrong with even the strictest of routines.

The following chart is from the diary of a mother with a five-week-old baby going approximately four hours between feeds. It shows how quickly things can go wrong, even when a strict four-hourly routine is followed.

Tues	3am	7am	11am	3pm	7pm	11pm
Wed	3am	7am	11am	3pm	7pm	11pm
Thurs	4am	8am	12pm	4pm	8pm	12am
Fri	5am	9am	1pm	5pm	9pm	11pm
Sat	2am	6am	10am	2pm	6pm	10pm
Sun	2am	6am	10am	2pm	6pm	10pm

Aware that the feeding pattern was going haywire, the mother tried to get it back on track on the Friday night by waking the baby up at 11pm. This did not work as the baby had taken a full feed at 9pm and was not hungry. It resulted in such a poor feed that the baby woke up at 2am needing a full feed, which meant a total backtrack on night feeding. Even if the mother had manged to settle the baby at 9pm with a smaller feed it is unlikely the baby would have fed any better. The baby had only been asleep for one hour so it would have been very difficult to wake him up enough to feed properly.

As I mentioned earlier the easiest way to keep your baby on track is to wake him at 7am. Once he is sleeping to 5am or 6am he should be offered a top-up feed at 7am or 7.30am. This method will not only keep the rest of your feeds on track, but ensure that your baby's sleeping is kept on track as well, and that he is ready to go to bed at 7pm. The following advice will also ensure that your baby sleeps through the night as soon as he is physically able, and prepare him for the introduction of solids and the eventual reduction of milk feeds.

Understanding the routine for feeding

The 6am–7am feed

Depending on what time he fed in the night, your baby will probably wake up between 6am and 7am, but he should always be woken at 7am regardless. It is important to remember that one of the main keys to getting your baby to sleep through the night is to ensure that once he is physically capable of taking bigger feeds, he takes his daily requirements between 7am and 11pm.

If he has had a full feed between 5am and 6am he will need a top-up by 7.30am, to keep his feeding and sleeping times on track. If he has slept to 5am or 6am and you do not give him the top-up feed, he will get hungry nearer 9am and not settle for his nap. This will have the knock-on effect of altering the times for all his naps and feeds. Regardless of whether they are breast or bottle fed, the only way to keep babies in a good routine is to begin the day at 7am. Once he is sleeping through the night he should be at his hungriest at this feed. If your baby is over two months, gaining 6–8oz each week and still feeding in the night but cutting back hard on this feed, it would be advisable to try and encourage him to cut out his middle of the night feed. Try offering him some cool boiled water when he wakes; if he refuses to settle then try to settle him with the smallest milk feed possible. During growth spurts, breast-fed babies should be given longer on the second breast, or if you are expressing at 6.45am reduce this by 30ml (1oz). Formula-fed babies should have their feeds increased by 30ml (1oz) when they are regularly draining their bottle.

By seven months

If your baby is eating a full breakfast of cereal, fruit and perhaps some small pieces of toast, you should aim to cut back the amount offered to him from the bottle. Try to divide his 240ml (8oz) feed so that half is given with the cereal and half as drink. Offer him his drink first at this meal. If you are still breastfeeding offer one breast, then the solids and finally the other breast. Your baby still needs a minimum of 600ml (20oz) a day inclusive of milk used in cooking or on cereal, divided between three to four milk feeds.

By ten months

If your baby is formula fed, try to encourage him to take all his milk from a cup. Ensure that you still offer milk at the start of the meal. Once he has taken a couple of ounces of milk, offer him some cereal. Then offer the milk again. It is important that he has at least 180–210ml (6–7oz) of milk divided between his cup and his breakfast cereal. If you are still breast feeding, offer him the first breast then his solids, then offer the second breast. Your baby needs a minimum of 500ml (17oz) a day inclusive of milk used in cooking or on cereal, divided between two or three milk feeds.

The 10am–11am feed

During the first few weeks, the majority of babies who have fed between 6am and 7am will wake looking for a feed around 10am. Even if your baby does not wake looking for a feed it is important that you wake him – ignore any comments about it being cruel to wake a sleeping baby. Remember that the aim is to ensure that your baby feeds regularly during the day so that he only needs to wake once for a feed between 11pm and 6–7am. In the early days many babies would happily sleep four to five hours between feeds during the day. Regardless of whether they are breast fed or bottle fed, within a very short period of time this usually leads to several night-time feeds as the baby attempts to make up his daily nutritional needs. Too few feeds during the day in the early weeks also does little to help establish a good

milk supply for a breast-feeding mother, and the baby feeding several times a night soon becomes so exhausting for the
mother that her milk supply is reduced even further.

Around four weeks he may show signs of being happy to
go longer from the 7am feed, and the 10am feed can gradually
be pushed to 10.30am. However, a baby who is feeding at
5am or 6am in the morning and being topped up at 7.30am
would probably still need to feed at 10am, as would the baby
who has too small a feed at 7am.

Once he is sleeping through the night or taking only a
small feed in the night, he should have the biggest feed of the
day at 7am (as discussed on page 110). If he feeds well he
should be happy to last until 11am before needing another
feed. However, if you feed him before he really needs it, he
may not feed well and as a result he may sleep poorly at his
lunchtime nap. This will have a knock on effect so that each
subsequent feed and nap has to be given earlier and may
result in the baby waking up at 6am or earlier the following
morning. This feed would be the next one to be increased
during growth spurts.

By five to six months

When your baby is eating breakfast you can start to make the
10–11am feed later, eventually settling somewhere between
11.30am and 12 noon. This will be the pattern for three
meals a day at six months, at which stage the milk feed will
be replaced with a drink of well-diluted juice or water from
a cup. Therefore, it is important that you introduce the tier
system of feeding so that he gradually cuts back on the milk
feed and increases his solids.

There are some babies who simply refuse to cut back on
this milk feed. If you find that your baby is one please refer
to Chapter 7 for suggestions on how to deal with this.

By six to seven months

When your baby is on a proper balanced diet of solids, which
includes solids protein with his lunch, it is important that the
10–11am feed should be replaced with a drink of water or

well-diluted juice. Milk given with a protein meal can reduce the iron absorption by up to 50 per cent. Give him most of his solids before his drink so he does not fill up with liquid first.

The 2.30pm feed

During the first few months I recommend that you make this feed smaller so that your baby feeds properly at the 5–6.15pm feed. If for some reason the baby fed badly at the 2pm feed or fed earlier, you should increase this feed accordingly so that he maintains his daily milk quota.

If your baby is very hungry and regularly drains his bottle at this feed then you can give him the full amount, provided he does not take less at the next feed. For breast-fed babies allow longer on the second breast if they are not getting through to the next feed happily.

By six to seven months

When your baby is having three full solid meals a day and his lunchtime milk feed has been replaced with water or well-diluted juice, you will probably need to increase the 2.30pm feed so he is getting his daily milk quota in three milk feeds. However, if he cuts back on his last milk feed of the day it would be advisable to keep this milk feed smaller and make up his daily quota by using milk in cereals and cooking. He still needs a minimum of 600ml (20oz) a day, inclusive of milk used on breakfast cereal and in cooking.

By nine to twelve months

Bottle-fed babies should be given their milk from a cup at this stage, which should automatically result in a decrease in the amount he drinks. However, if this is not the case and he starts to lose interest in his morning or evening feed, you could cut right back on this feed. If he is getting 530ml (18oz) of milk a day (inclusive of milk used in cooking and on cereal), plus a full, balanced diet of solids you could cut this food altogether. Refer to page 217 for details of what constitutes a full, balanced diet at this age. By one year of age he needs a minimum of 350ml (12oz) a day, inclusive of milk used in cooking and on cereal.

The 6–7pm feed

It is important that your baby always has a good feed at this time if you want him to settle well between 7pm and 10–11pm. He should not be fed milk after 3.15pm as it could put him off taking a really good feed at this time. I advise that in the first few weeks this feed is split between 5pm and 6.15pm so that the baby is not getting too frantic during his bath. Once your baby has slept through the night for two weeks the 5pm feed can be dropped. I would not recommend dropping the split feed until this happens as a larger feed at 6.15pm could result in your baby taking even less at the late feed, resulting in an earlier waking time. Breast-fed babies not settling at 7pm should be offered a top-up of expressed milk.

By four to five months

Most babies drop their late feed by this stage, so the 6–7pm feed will be the last one of the day. As a consequence you should ensure that it is an adequate one. A baby on solids should be given most of his milk before his solids, as milk is still the most important form of nutrition at this age.

Most babies would be taking at least 210–240ml (7–8oz) of formula at this age, and a breast fed baby would need to be fed from both breasts. If he cuts back or plays up at this feed then cut right back on his 2.30pm feed. If he is very tired at this feed and you are struggling to get him to take all of his milk feed plus his solids I would advise adjusting the feeding times. Try giving two-thirds of his milk feed at around 5.45pm followed by his solids, then delay his bath to around 6.25pm. After the bath he can then be offered the remainder of his milk feed. If formula feeding it is advisable to make up two separate bottles to ensure that the milk is fresh.

A breast-fed baby who reaches five months, is weaned, and still looking for a milk feed at 10pm may not be getting enough at this time. Try giving both breasts at 5.45pm followed by the solids, with a bath at 6.25pm followed by a top-up of expressed milk or formula after the bath.

By six to seven months

Most babies will now be having tea at 5pm followed by a 210–240ml (7–8oz) bottle or both breasts at 6.30pm. If your baby starts to take less at this feed and is waking earlier in the morning, go back to giving him most or all of his milk first. Continue this for a couple of weeks before trying the solids at 5pm again.

By ten to twelve months

It is important that bottle-fed babies are taking all of their milk from a cup at one year. Babies who continue to feed from a bottle after this age are more prone to feeding problems, as they continue to take large amounts which takes the edge of their appetite for solids. They can also become very attached to the bottle and it can be very difficult to get them to give up at a later stage.

Start encouraging your baby to take some of his milk from a cup, so that by that one year he is happy to take all of his last feed from a cup.

The 10–11pm feed

I strongly advise all parents of breast-fed babies to introduce a bottle of either expressed milk or formula at this feed, no later than the second week. All of the babies I helped care for were given a bottle feed of either expressed milk or formula at this time, and I am convinced that it is one of the reasons that I only ever had to get up once in the night to them. It also avoids the very common problem of babies refusing to take a bottle at a later stage. A totally breast-fed baby under three months who continues to wake up between 2am and 3am and shows no sign of going a longer spell in the night may not be getting enough to eat at this time, as the breast milk supply is often at its lowest at this time of day.

If you choose to top up with expressed milk or formula rather than completely replace the feed with a full bottle feed, it is essential that you ensure your baby is encouraged to empty both breasts before being offered the bottle.

With formula-fed babies it is easier to tell whether they are getting enough to eat at this feed. If you always increase the day feeds during your baby's growth spurts, he will probably never require more than 180ml (6oz) at this feed. However, some babies who weighed more than 10lb at birth may reach a stage where they need more than this. Refer to page 63 for guidelines on how much formula your baby needs to drink each day.

By three to four months

If your baby has slept through the night until 7am for at least two weeks then I recommend that you bring the 10–11pm feed forward by 10 minutes every three nights, until your baby is sleeping from 10pm to 7am. If your baby is totally breast fed and is still waking up in the night despite being topped up with expressed milk at the late feed, it may be worthwhile replacing the late breast feed with a formula feed. Most formula-fed babies will be taking 210–240ml (7–8oz) a feed four times a day, and will only want a small feed of 120–180ml (4–6oz) at this time of night. However, if your formula-fed baby is not sleeping through the night at this age it may be because he needs a little extra at this feed, and even if it means he cuts back on his morning feed it may be worthwhile offering him an extra ounce or two. Some babies simply refuse the 10–11pm feed at three to four months. If your baby is feeding well from both breasts four times a day, or taking a minimum of 600ml (20oz) of formula a day, you can just drop this feed – provided his weekly weight gain is still between 4–6oz a week.

By four to five months

At this age the majority of babies should be capable of sleeping through the night from their last feed provided they are taking their daily intake of milk between 7am and 11pm. I usually find that once the baby is taking around three teaspoonfuls of baby rice mixed with either formula or breast milk at the 6pm feed, you should be able to gradually cut back on this last feed. If you do not do this your baby will not feed so well in the morning. With formula-fed babies, cut back this feed by 30ml (1oz) every three nights. With those fully breast fed cut back feeding time by two minutes each side. If your baby continues to sleep through on a 60ml (2oz) formula feed or three minutes each breast for a further three nights, you should find that you can drop this feed without him waking during the night.

The 2am–3am feed

Newborn babies need to feed little and often during the first week, so when he wakes it is best to assume that he is hungry and feed him. A newborn baby should never be allowed to go longer than three hours between feeds during the day and four hours between feeds in the night. Once your baby has regained his birth weight he should start to settle into the 2–4 week routine. Provided he feeds well between 10pm and 11pm he should manage to get to nearer 2am.

By four to six weeks

Most babies weighing over 7lb at birth and gaining a regular 6–8oz each week are capable of lasting a longer stretch between feeds during the night as long as:

a) The baby is definitely over 9lb in weight and taking his daily allowance of milk in the five feeds between 7am and 11pm.
b) The baby is not sleeping more than 4 1/2 hours between 7am and 7pm.

By six to eight weeks

If your baby is over 9lb in weight and gaining 6–8oz each week, but is still waking between 2am and 3am, despite taking a good feed between 10pm and 11pm, I recommend that you try to settle him with some cool, boiled water. If he refuses to settle then you will have to feed him, but it would be advisable to refer to Chapter 4 to check for possible reasons why he is not going longer in the night.

If he does settle he will probably wake up again around 5am, at which time you can give him a full feed, followed by a top-up at 7–7.30am. This will help keep him on track with his feeding and sleeping pattern for the rest of the day. Within a week I normally find that babies are sleeping until nearer 5am, gradually increasing their sleep time until 7am. During this stage when the baby is taking a top-up at 7–7.30am instead of a full feed he may not manage to get through to 10.45–11am for his next feed. Therefore, I would advise that you give him half a feed at 10am followed by the remainder at the usual time.

By three to four months

Both breast-fed and bottle-fed babies should be able to go one long spell during the night, provided they are getting their daily intake of milk between 6–7am and 10–11pm at night. They should also be sleeping no more than three hours between 7am and 7pm. If your baby insists on waking up in the night, refuses cool, boiled water and will not settle without feeding it would be advisable to keep a very detailed diary listing exact times and amounts of feeding and times of daytime naps. A baby who cuts right back on his 7am is probably waking out of habit rather than hunger. If you allowed this to continue you would end up with your baby dropping his 7am feed and going the longest stretch at the wrong time.

Some breast-fed babies may still genuinely need to feed in the night if they are not getting enough at their last feed. If this is the case he would feed in the night and then feed well again from both breasts in the morning. If you are not already doing so, it is worth considering a top-up feed at either 6.15pm or at the 10–11pm feed.

Regardless of whether you are breast feeding or bottle feeding, if your baby's weight gain is good and you are convinced he is waking up from habit and refuses cool, boiled water I would try leaving it for 15–20 minutes before going to him. Some babies will actually settle themselves back to sleep. I would then try with the cool, boiled water and only resort to feeding if the baby absolutely refused to settle.

Another reason a baby of this age may be still be waking up in the night is because he is getting out of his covers. I would suggest tucking him in using two rolled-up towels wedged between the mattress and the spars of the cot to keep the sheet firm.

By four to five months

If, when he reaches nearly five months and is weaned, your baby still persists in waking in the night I would try the method Richard Ferber suggests. If you gradually dilute the middle-of-the-night feed with water a little more every few nights, your baby will increase his daytime intake of milk. This would reduce any genuine need for milk in the night. For night-time waking it would be wise to consider a sleep training programme before a long-term sleep problem evolves. Before embarking on a sleep training programme it is important that you have your baby checked over by your doctor to ensure that there are no medical reasons for the night waking, or any reasons that would prevent you embarking on the sleep training programme. Sleep training is described more fully in my problem solver book *From Contented Baby to Confident Child.*

Milk feeding chart for the first year

Age	Times
2–4 weeks	2–3am 6–7am 10–10.30am 2–2.30am 5pm 6–6.30pm 10–11pm
4–6 weeks	3–4am 6–7am 10.30–11am 2–2.30pm 5pm 6–6.30pm 10–11pm
6–8 weeks	4–5am 7.30am 10.45–11am 2–2.30pm 6–6.30pm 10–11pm
8–10 weeks	5–6am 7.30am 11am 2–2.30pm 6–6.30pm 10–11pm
10–12 weeks	7am 11am 2–2.30pm 6–6.30pm 10–11pm
3–4 months	7am 11am 2–2.30pm 6–6.30pm 10–10.30pm
4–5 months	7am 11am 2–2.30pm 6–6.30pm 10pm
5–6 months	7am 11.30am 2–2.30pm 6–6.30pm
6–7 months	7am 2–2.30pm 6–6.30pm
7–8 months	7am 2–2.30pm 6–6.30pm
8–9 months	7am 2–2.30pm 6–6.30pm
9–10 months	7am 5pm 6.30–7pm
10–12 months	7am 5pm 6.30–7pm

Structuring daytime sleep during the first year

To ensure good night-time sleep for your baby it is essential that you structure his daytime sleep. Too much daytime sleep can result in night-time wakings. Too little daytime sleep can result in an overtired, irritable baby who has difficulty settling himself to sleep, and who falls asleep only when he is totally exhausted. Infant sleep expert Marc Weissbluth (see page 99) has done extensive research into the nap patterns of more than 200 children. He says that napping is one of the health habits that sets the stage for good overall sleep and explains that a nap offers the baby a break from stimuli and allows him to recharge for further activity. Charles Schaefer PhD, professor of psychology at Fairleigh Dickinson University in Teaneck, New Jersey, supports this and says: 'Naps structure the day, shape both the baby's and the mother's moods, and offer the only opportunity for Mom to relax or accomplish a few tasks.'

Several leading experts on child care are in agreement that naps are essential to a baby's brain development. John Herman PhD, infant sleep expert and associate professor of psychology and psychiatry at the University of Texas, says: 'If activities are being scheduled to the detriment of sleep, it's a mistake. Parents should remember that everything else in a baby's life should come after sleeping and eating.' I would agree totally with this new research and could have confirmed their findings years ago, down to the very times they suggest babies should take their naps.

By three to four months most babies are capable of sleeping 12 hours at night, provided their daytime sleep is no more than three to three and a half hours, divided between two or three naps a day. If you want your baby to sleep from 7/7.30pm to 7/7.30am, it is very important that you structure these naps so that he has his longest nap at midday, with two shorter ones – one in the morning and one late afternoon. While it may be more convenient to let your baby have a longer nap in the morning followed by a shorter nap in the afternoon, this can lead to problems as he gets older.

Once he reduces his daytime sleep naturally he is most likely to cut back on his late afternoon nap. His longest nap of the day would then be in the morning. By late afternoon he will be exhausted and need to go to bed by 6.30pm. This has a knock-on effect, which results in him waking up at 6am. If you manage to get him to have a nap in the late afternoon you could then be faced with the problem of him not settling well at 7/7.30pm.

Understanding the sleeping routine

Morning nap

Most babies are ready for a nap approximately two hours from the time they wake up in the morning. This should always be a short nap of around 45 minutes. Between 12 and 18 months they may reduce the time of the nap or cut it out all together. You will know your baby is ready to drop this nap when he starts taking a long time to settle, and ends up only sleeping 10–15minutes of his 45-minute nap. If this continues for a couple of weeks and he manages to get through to his lunch-time nap happily, cut out the morning nap altogether. It is very important that you always start to wake him up after the 45-minute period, even if he has only slept for ten minutes. If you allow him to sleep past this time you will not know whether he is ready to drop the nap. It could also cause him to sleep too little at his lunch-time nap, which could result in the problems that I discussed earlier.

Six weeks onwards

Never allow your baby to sleep more than 45 minutes, as it may result in a shorter lunch-time nap. This will have a knock-on effect on the rest of his sleep, resulting in an early morning waking. Until a proper sleep pattern has been established, try to ensure that this nap takes place in his nursery, in the dark, with the door shut. Once a proper daytime routine has been established, this nap could at times be taken in the buggy or car seat if you have to go out, but do remember to wake him after the 45 minutes.

Six months onwards

If your baby is on three meals a day, the morning nap may be pushed to 9.30am. You will know your baby is ready for this if he consistently and continually chatters for 30 minutes or so when you put him down. This nap may need to be cut back to 20–30 minutes if he is sleeping less than two hours at lunch time from 12 months onwards.

If he is awake at 7am he may still need a short nap of 30 minutes at 9.30am. If you find he is only sleeping 10–15 minutes out of the 45-minute nap time and is getting through happily to his lunch-time nap you could cut it out altogether. If he sleeps to 8am he should be able to get through to his lunch-time nap, without the morning nap.

Lunch-time nap

This should always be the longest nap of the day. By establishing a good lunch-time nap you will ensure that your baby is not too tired to enjoy afternoon activities, and that bedtime is relaxed and happy. Recent research shows that a nap between noon and 2pm is deeper and more refreshing than a later nap because it coincides with the baby's natural dip in alertness. As I explained earlier, allowing a longer nap in the morning, followed by a shorter nap at this time will in turn affect the rest of his sleep, which can result in an early morning awakening.

Most babies will need a sleep of two to two and a half hours until they are two years of age, when it will gradually reduce to one to one and a half hours. By three years of age they may not need a sleep after lunch, but they should always be encouraged to have some quiet time in their room.

Otherwise, they are likely to get very hyperactive by late afternoon, which can affect the night sleep.

Six weeks onwards

If your baby is sleeping the full 45 minutes in the morning, he should be woken after 2 1/4 hours at lunch time. If for some reason his morning nap was much shorter then you could allow him 2 1/2 hours. If your baby develops a problem with his night-time sleep do not make the mistake of letting him sleep longer during the day.

In the early days a lunch-time nap may sometimes go wrong and your baby will refuse to go back to sleep. Obviously he cannot make it through from 1pm to 4pm happily. I find the best way to deal with this is to allow 30 minutes after the 2.30pm feed, then a further 30 minutes at 4.30pm. This should stop him getting overtired and irritable and get things back on track so that he goes to sleep well at 7pm.

Six months onwards

If your baby is on three meals a day or you have moved the morning nap from 9am to 9.30am, he will most likely need to adjust the lunch-time nap to 12.30pm–2.30pm. If he is sleeping less than two hours at lunch time, check that his morning nap between 7am and 12 noon is no more than 45 minutes.

Twelve months onwards

If your baby has difficulty in settling for the nap or is waking up after one to one and a half hours, you might have to cut the morning nap right back or cut it out altogether. Do not let him sleep after 2.30 in the afternoon if you want him to go to sleep at 7pm.

Late afternoon nap

This is the shortest nap of the three, and the one the baby should drop first. It is not essential that your baby goes in his cot for this nap. It is a good idea occasionally to let him catnap in his buggy or chair for this nap, as it allows you the freedom to get out and about.

Three months onwards

If you want your baby to go to sleep at 7pm he should never sleep more than 45 minutes at the late afternoon nap, and he should always be awake by 5pm regardless of how long or short his sleep was. Most babies who are sleeping well at the other two naps will gradually cut back on this sleep until they cut it out altogether. If for some reason his lunch-time nap was cut short you would need to allow him a short sleep now, but ensure that the daily total does not exceed the amount needed for his age.

Adjusting the routines

Birth to four months

I have tried many different routines over the years and without exception I have found the 7am to 7pm routine to be the one in which tiny babies and young infants are happiest. It fits in with their natural sleep rhythms and their need to feed little and often. I urge parents to try and stick to the original routine whenever possible. Once your baby reaches the age of four months, is on four feeds a day and needs less sleep, it is possible to change the routine without affecting your baby's natural needs for the right amount of sleep and number of feeds.

Up to the age of four months the following points should be noted when planning a routine:

- In the very early weeks, to avoid more than one waking in the night, you must fit in at least five feeds before midnight. This can only be done if your baby starts his day at 6am or 7am.
- An 8am to 8pm routine in the first few weeks would mean your baby would end up feeding twice between midnight and 7am.

Four months onwards

From four months most babies who have started solids will have dropped their late-night feed. It is then easier to adjust the routine. If your baby has been sleeping regularly to 7am it could be possible to change to a 7.30am or 8am start, and push the rest of the routine forward. Your baby would obviously need to go to sleep later in the evenings. If you want your baby to sleep later but still go to bed at 7pm, try the following:

- Cut right back on the morning nap, so that your baby is ready to go to bed at 12–12.30pm.
- Allow a nap of no longer than two hours at lunch-time and no late afternoon nap.

Out and about

In the first few weeks most young babies will go to sleep the minute they are in the car or the buggy. If possible, try to organize shopping trips during the sleep times so that the routine is not too disrupted. Once the routine is established and your baby is nearer eight weeks you will find that you are able to go out more without him falling asleep the whole time.

If you are planning a day visit to friends, depending on the length of the visit, you can usually work it into the routine by travelling between 9am and 10am or 1pm and 2pm. By the time you arrive at the destination the baby will be due for a feed and can be kept awake. Likewise, by making the return journey between 4pm and 5pm or after 7pm you should manage to keep things on track.

Sleep required during the first year

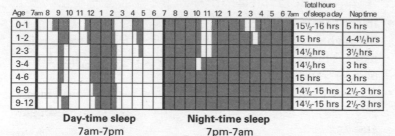

Age	7am 8 9 10 11 12 1 2 3 4 5 6 7 8 9 10 11 12 1 2 3 4 5 6 7am	Total hours of sleep a day	Nap time
0-1		15½-16 hrs	5 hrs
1-2		15 hrs	4-4½ hrs
2-3		14½ hrs	3½ hrs
3-4		14½ hrs	3 hrs
4-6		15 hrs	3 hrs
6-9		14½-15 hrs	2½-3 hrs
9-12		14½-15 hrs	2½-3 hrs

Day-time sleep
7am-7pm

Night-time sleep
7pm-7am

Routines for the first year | 7

Routine for a breast-feeding baby at one week

Feed times	Nap times between 7am and 7pm
7am	8.30–10am
10am–11.15am	11.30–2pm
2pm	3.30–5pm
5pm	
6.15pm	
10–11.15pm	**Maximum daily sleep 5 1/2 hours**

Expressing times: 6.45am, 10.45am and 10pm

7am
- Baby should be awake, nappy changed and feeding no later than 7am.
- He needs 25–35 minutes on the full breast, then offered 10–15 minutes on the second breast after you have expressed 60–90ml (2–3oz).
- If he fed at 5am or 6am, offer 20–25 minutes from the second breast after expressing 90ml (3oz).
- **Do not feed after 8am, as it will put baby off his next feed.** He can stay awake for up to one and a half hours.

8am
- You should have cereal, toast and a drink no later than 8am.

8.15am
- Baby should start to get a bit sleepy by this time. **Even if he does not show signs, he will be getting tired, so take him to his room now.** Check his nappy and draw sheet and close the curtains.

8.30am
- **Before he is asleep or before he goes into a deep sleep, settle baby in his cot, fully swaddled (see page 27) in the dark with the door shut, no later than 9am.** He needs a sleep of no longer than one and a half hours.
- Wash and sterilize bottles and expressing equipment.

9.45am
- Open the curtains and unswaddle the baby so that he can wake up naturally.
- Prepare things for top-and-tailing and dressing.

10am
- **Baby must be fully awake now, regardless of how long he slept.**
- He should be given 25–35 minutes from the breast he last fed on while you drink a large glass of water.
- Lay him in his Moses basket or cot so he can have a good kick and doesn't become too sleepy, while you prepare equipment for expressing.

10.45am
- Express 60ml (2oz) from the second breast.
- Wash and dress baby, remembering to cream all his creases.

11am
- He should then be offered 15–20 minutes from the breast you have just expressed from.

11.20am
- Baby should start to get a bit sleepy by this time. **Even if he does not show the signs, he will be getting tired, so take him to his room now.** Check the draw sheet and change his nappy.

- Close the curtains and settle baby once he is drowsy, fully swaddled and in the dark with the door shut, no later than 11.30am.
- If he doesn't settle within ten minutes, offer him ten minutes from the fullest breast. Do this in the dark with no talking or eye contact.

11.30am – 2pm
- Baby needs a nap of no longer than two and a half hours from the time he went down.
- **If he wakes up after 45 minutes check the swaddle, but do not talk to him or turn the lights on.**
- **Allow ten minutes for him to resettle himself;** if he's still unsettled offer him half his 2pm feed and try to settle him back to sleep until 2pm.

12noon
- Wash and sterilize expressing equipment, then you should have lunch and rest before the next feed.

2pm
- **Baby must be awake and feeding no later than 2pm, regardless of how long he has slept.**
- Open the curtains, unswaddle him and allow him to wake up naturally. Change his nappy.
- Give 25–35 minutes from the breast he last fed on. If he is still hungry offer 10–15 minutes from the other breast while you drink a large glass of water.
- **Do not feed after 3.15pm, as it will put him off his next feed.**
- **It is very important that he is fully awake now until 3.30pm, so he goes down well at 7pm;** if he was very alert in the morning he may be more sleepy now. Do not put too many clothes on him, as extra warmth will make him drowsy.

3.30pm
- Change baby's nappy. This is a good time to take him for a walk to ensure that he sleeps well, and is refreshed for his bath and next feed.

- Baby should not sleep after 5pm if you want him to go down well at 7pm.

5pm
- Baby must be fully awake and feeding no later than 5pm.
- Give him a good 25–30 minutes on the breast he last fed on.
- It is very important that he is not dozy while feeding and that he is not allowed the other breast until after his bath.

5.45pm
- If baby has been very wakeful during the day or didn't nap well between 3.30pm and 5pm, he may need to start his bath early.
- Allow him a good kick without his nappy while preparing things needed for his bath and bedtime.

6pm
- Baby must start his bath no later than 6pm, and be massaged and dressed by 6.15pm.

6.15pm
- Baby must be feeding no later than 6.15pm; this should be done in the nursery with dim lights and no talking or eye contact.
- If he did not empty the first breast at 5pm, give him 5–10 minutes on it before putting him on the full breast. Allow a good 20-25 minutes on the full breast.
- It is very important that baby is in bed two hours from when he last awoke.

7pm
- When he becomes drowsy settle him fully swaddled and in the dark, with the door shut, no later than 7pm.
- If he doesn't settle within 10-15 minutes, offer him ten minutes from the fullest breast. Do this in the dark with no talking or eye contact.

8pm
- It is very important that you have a really good meal and a rest before the next feed or expressing.

9.45pm

- Turn the lights on fully and unswaddle baby so that he can wake up naturally. Allow at least ten minutes before feeding to ensure that he is fully awake, so that he can feed well.
- Lay out things for the nappy change, plus a spare draw sheet, muslin and swaddle blanket in case they are needed in the middle of the night.
- Give him 25–35 minutes from the breast he last fed on or most of his bottle feed, change his nappy and re-swaddle him.
- **Then dim the lights and with no talking or eye contact, give him 20-25 minutes on the second breast or the remainder of his bottle feed. This feed should take no longer than one hour.**

In the night

During the second week it is important that breast-fed babies are not allowed to go too long in the night between feeds. A baby weighing less than 7lb at birth should be woken around 2.30am for a feed, and a baby weighing between 7lb and 8lb should be woken no later than 3.30am. A formula-fed baby who weighs more than 8lb who has fed well during the day may be able to go slightly longer, but not any longer than five hours. If you are in doubt as to how long to allow your baby to sleep between feeds in the night, please seek advice from your paediatrician or health visitor.

Advancing to the two- to four-week routine

By the end of the second week a baby should have regained his birth weight and provided he now weighs over 7lb, you should be able to advance onto the two- to four- week routine.

The following signs will help you decide whether you can advance onto the two- to four-week routine:

- Your baby should weigh over 7lb, have regained his birth weight and show signs of gaining approximately an ounce a day in weight.
- He is sleeping well at nap times and more often than not you have to wake him from his naps for him to be fed.
- He is feeding more efficiently and often emptying a breast within 25-30 minutes.
- He is showing signs of being more alert and managing to stay awake easily for an hour and a half at time.

Routine for a breast-feeding baby at two to four weeks

Feed times	Nap times between 7am and 7pm
7am	8.30/9am–10am
10am	11.30/12 noon–2pm
2pm	4–5pm
5pm	
6.15pm	
10.30pm	**Maximum daily sleep 5 hours**
Expressing times: 6.45am, 9.45am and 10pm	

7am
- Baby should be awake, nappy changed and feeding no later than 7am.
- He needs 20–25 minutes on the full breast, then 10–15 minutes on the second breast after you have expressed 60–90ml (2–3oz).
- If he fed at 5am or 6am offer 20–25 minutes from the second breast after expressing 90ml (3oz).
- Do not feed after 7.45am, as it will put baby off his next feed. He can stay awake for up to two hours.

8am
- You should have cereal, toast and a drink no later than 8am.

8.45am
- Baby should start to get a bit sleepy by this time. Even if he does not show the signs, he will be getting tired, so take him to his room now. Check his nappy and draw sheet and close the curtains.

9am
- Before he is asleep or before he goes into a deep sleep, settle baby in his cot, fully swaddled (see page 27), in the dark with the door shut, no later than 9am. He needs a sleep of no longer than one and a half hours.
- Wash and sterilize bottles and expressing equipment.

9.45am
- Open the curtains and unswaddle baby so that he can wake up naturally.
- Prepare things for top-and-tailing and dressing.

10am
- Baby must be fully awake now, regardless of how long he slept.
- He should be given 20–25 minutes from the breast he last fed on while you drink a large glass of water.
- Wash and dress baby, remembering to cream all his creases.

10.30am
- Express 60ml (2oz) from the second breast, then offer baby 10–15 minutes. Do not feed after 11.15am, as it will put him off his next feed.
- Lay him on his play mat so that he can have a good kick before he gets too tired.

11.30am
- If baby was very alert and awake during the previous two hours, he may start to get tired by 11.30am and would need to be in bed by 11.45am.

11.45am
- Regardless of what he has done earlier he should now be taken to his room.
- Check the draw sheet and change his nappy.
- Close the curtains and settle baby once he is drowsy, fully swaddled and in the dark with the door shut, no later than 12 noon.

11.30/12 noon–2pm
- Baby needs a nap of no longer than two and a half hours from the time he went down.
- If he slept one and a half hours earlier, only allow him two hours this nap time.
- If he wakes up after 45 minutes check the swaddle, but do not talk to him or turn the lights on.
- Allow 20 minutes for him to resettle himself; if he's still unsettled offer him half his 2pm feed and try to settle him back to sleep until 2pm.

12 noon
- Wash and sterilize expressing equipment, then you should have lunch and rest before the next feed.

2pm
- Baby must be awake and feeding no later than 2pm, regardless of how long he has slept.
- Open the curtains, unswaddle him and allow him to wake up naturally. Change his nappy.
- Give 20–25 minutes from the breast he last fed on. If he is still hungry offer 10–15 minutes from the other breast while you drink a large glass of water.
- Do not feed after 3.15pm as it will put him off his next feed.
- It is very important that he is fully awake now until 4pm, so he goes down well at 7pm; if he was very alert in the morning he may be more sleepy now. Do not put too many clothes on him, as extra warmth will make him drowsy.
- Lay him on his play mat and encourage him to have a good kick.

4pm
- Change baby's nappy. This is a good time to take him for a walk to ensure that he sleeps well, and is refreshed for his bath and next feed.
- Baby should not sleep after 5pm if you want him to go down well at 7pm.

5pm
- Baby must be fully awake and feeding no later than 5pm.
- Give him a good 20 minutes on the breast he last fed on.
- It is very important that he is not allowed the other breast until after his bath.

5.45pm
- If baby has been very wakeful during the day or didn't nap well between 4pm and 5pm, he may need to start his bath early.
- Allow him a good kick without his nappy while preparing things needed for his bath and bedtime.

6pm
- Baby must start his bath no later than 6pm, and be massaged and dressed by 6.15pm.

6.15pm
- Baby must be feeding no later than 6.15pm; this should be done in the nursery with dim lights and no talking or eye contact.
- If he did not empty the first breast at 5pm, allow 5–10 minutes before putting him on the full breast and give him a good 20–25 minutes on it.
- It is very important that baby is in bed two hours from when he last awoke.

7pm
- When he becomes drowsy settle him, fully swaddled and in the dark, with the door shut, no later than 7pm.
- If he doesn't settle within 10–15 minutes, offer him ten minutes from the fullest breast. Do this in the dark with no talking or eye contact.

8pm
- It is very important that you have a really good meal and a rest before the next feed or expressing.

10/10.30pm
- Turn on the lights fully and unswaddle baby so that he can wake up naturally. Allow at least ten minutes before feeding to ensure he is fully awake, so that he can feed well.
- Lay out things for the nappy change, plus a spare draw sheet, muslin and swaddle blanket in case they are needed in the middle of the night.
- Give him 20 minutes from the breast he last fed on or most of his formula feed, change his nappy and re-swaddle him.
- Then dim the lights and with no talking or eye contact give him 20 minutes on the second breast or the remainder of the formula feed. This feed should take no longer than one hour.

In the night
- If baby wakes before 4am give him a full feed.
- If he wakes between 4am and 5am give him one breast, then the second at 7am after expressing.
- If he wakes at 6am give him one breast, then the second at 7.30am after expressing.
- Make sure that you keep the lights dim and avoid eye contact or talking. Only change his nappy if absolutely necessary.

Changes to be made during the two- to four-week routine

Sleep

By three to four weeks your baby should start to show signs of being more wakeful and for longer periods. Ensure that you encourage this wakefulness during the day so that his night-time sleep is not affected. If possible, try to continue to put him in the nursery in the dark with the door shut for all his daytime sleeps, except the 4pm one. If school runs with older children prevent this, try at least to put him down for his lunch-time nap in his nursery in the dark. Between 7pm and 7am he should always be put down in the nursery and in the dark, with the door shut. By four weeks the morning nap should be no more than one hour, to ensure that he sleeps well at lunch-time. Gradually, aim to keep him awake longer in the morning, until he is going down for his sleep at 9am. If you find that he is going to sleep at 8.30am and waking up between 9.15am and 9.30am, which has an adverse affect on the rest of the day, topping and tailing him around 8.20am is usually enough to revive him to last until 9am. If school runs prevent you from doing this and he is awake from 9.15am, you could try allowing him a short catnap of ten minutes around 10.45–11am. This means he would go down for his lunch-time nap somewhere between 12.15–12.30pm, avoiding the much earlier time of 11.15am if he had been awake since 9.15am. The lunch-time nap should be no more than two and a half hours and the after-noon nap no more than one hour in total: this nap is some-times broken into a couple of catnaps between 4pm and 5pm.

By four weeks he should be half swaddled (under the arms) for the 9am nap, and for the late afternoon nap. Around four weeks it becomes more obvious when the baby comes into his light sleep: normally every 45 minutes, although it can be every 30 minutes with some babies. If a feed is not due, most babies, given the opportunity, settle themselves back to sleep. Rushing too quickly to your baby and assisting him back to sleep by rocking, patting or using the dummy could result in a long-term sleep association problem. This means that in the night when your baby comes into his light sleep, you could end up getting up several times to help him back to sleep, long after the time he no longer needs night feeds.

Feeding

Most babies go through a growth spurt around the third week. When your baby goes through a growth spurt, reduce the amount you express at 6.45am by 30ml (1oz) and by the end of the fourth week reduce the 10.30am expressing by 30ml (1oz). This will ensure that your baby immediately receives the extra milk he needs. If you have not been expressing, you will need to allow your baby to feed more often on the breast and for longer periods so he is getting the amounts he needs. During this time try to get extra rest so that your baby's increased feeding demands do not have the opposite effect on you, causing you to become so exhausted that your milk supply decreases even further. If you do not wish to lose his sleeping routine, you could try using the plan on page 52, which increases the milk supply without losing the sleeping routine. Once your milk supply has increased, you can then go back to following the routine suitable for your baby's age.

If you are breast-feeding and have decided to give one bottle feed a day, this is a good age to introduce it. If you leave it any later than this age it is very possible that your baby will refuse a bottle altogether, which can cause enormous problems later on, particularly if you are going back to work. It is advisable to express somewhere between 9.30pm and 10pm; totally emptying both breasts to keep your milk supply up. This milk can either be used for the 10.30pm feed, or frozen and used on the occasions when you need to leave your baby with a babysitter. Introducing a bottle of either expressed milk or formula at 10.30pm also allows the father to get involved and enables the mother to get to bed earlier, giving her the much-needed extra sleep that all mothers need during the early weeks. If you wish to breast feed for longer than six weeks, avoid giving formula at any other feeds unless advised by your health visitor or paediatrician.

Bottle fed babies should have their 7am, 10.30am and 10.30pm feeds increased first during growth spurts. Some bottle-fed babies are ready to go from using a newborn teat to a slow flow teat.

Once your baby reaches four weeks he will probably show signs of being happy to go slightly longer between feeds, and you should be able to move him onto the four to six week feeding routine, provided he is regularly gaining 6–8oz each week. Breast-fed babies who are not gaining sufficient weight should remain on the two- to four-week routine until their weight gain improves. Low weight gain in breast-fed babies is usually caused by a low milk supply or poor positioning at the breast, the two usually going hand in hand. It would be worthwhile following the plan for increasing your milk supply on page 52. I would also advise that you arrange a home visit from a breast-feeding counsellor to check that you are positioning your baby on the breast correctly.

If your baby is formula fed and not gaining sufficient weight, try moving him from the newborn teat with one hole to the slow flow teat with two holes. Always discuss any concerns you have regarding your baby's low weight gain with your health visitor or paediatrician.

If you find your baby is still waking around 2am then again at 5am, I would suggest that you wake him promptly at 10pm, give him most of his feed and keep him awake for longer than the recommended one hour. At 11.15pm his nappy should be changed and the lights dimmed in his nursery while you give him a small top-up feed. By giving him a split feed and having him awake slightly longer at this time, he will more than likely sleep well past 3am, provided he is not getting out of his covers (see page 75).

Schedule for twins
at two to four weeks

Feed times	Nap times between 7am and 7pm
7am	8.30–10am
10am	1.30am–2/2.15pm
2/2.15pm	4–5pm
6pm	
10.30pm	**Maximum daily sleep 5 hours**

6.50am
- **One of the twins should be awake, nappy changed and feeding no later than 6.50am.**
- Offer at least 15 minutes on the breast before starting to wake the second baby.
- When the first baby has fed for 15–20 minutes, change the nappy of the second baby and start feeding.
- Once the second baby has fed for 20 minutes, go back and finish the feed of the first baby, then finish the feed of the second baby.
- **Do not feed after 8am, as it will put them off the next feed.**
- They can stay awake for up to two hours, but no longer.

8.20am
- The baby who awoke first should start to get a bit sleepy by this time. Always try to settle the baby who fed first to sleep at least 10–15 minutes before settling the second baby.

9am
- **Both babies should be settled in their cots, fully swaddled and in the dark with the door shut before they get into a deep sleep.**
- They need a sleep of no longer than one and a half hours.

9.45am
Open the curtains and unswaddle first baby; allow baby to wake up naturally.

10am

- The first baby should be given 10–15 minutes on the breast before unswaddling the second baby.
- Continue to feed the first baby until the second baby is fully awake.
- Once the second baby is fully awake, offer 20 minutes on the breast.
- Top and tail and dress the first baby, then offer the remainder of the feed.
- Top and tail and dress the second baby, then offer the remainder of the feed.
- Put them under the play gym or mobile so they can have a good kick before they get too tired.
- **Do not feed after 11.15am, as it will put them off the next feed.**

11.20am

- Regardless of how long they have slept earlier, they should be taken to their room now.
- Check draw sheet and change nappy, close blind and curtains.
- Settle the first baby fully swaddled in the cot, before fully swaddling and settling the second baby.
- **Both babies should be put in their cots before they get into a deep sleep, and no later than 12 noon.**

11.30am–2.00/2.15pm

- They need a nap of no longer than two and a half hours from the time they went down.
- **If either awakes after one hour, check swaddle but do not talk or turn the light on.**
- If still unsettled at 1.45pm, offer half the 2pm feed, and settle back to sleep.
- **Do this in the dark with no talking or eye contact.**

2pm

- Open the curtains and unswaddle the first baby. Once

awake, offer 15 minutes on the breast before unswaddling the second baby.

- The second baby should be awake and feeding no later than 2.15pm. Offer 15–20 minutes on the breast.
- Change the nappy of the first baby and finish feed, then change the nappy of the second baby and finish feed.
- **Do not feed after 3.15pm as it will put them off the next feed.**
- **Very important: they should be fully awake until 4pm, so they go down well at 7pm.**

3.30pm
- If they get very irritable and unable to stay awake, let them have a catnap of no more than 15 minutes. They should be awake by 4pm.

4.15pm
- Change babies' nappies. This is a good time to take them for a walk to ensure they sleep well, and are refreshed for their bath and next feed.

4.30pm
- **If they are still awake and had a catnap earlier, it is essential that they have a further 15 minutes before 5pm, otherwise they will be over-tired for the bath.**

5pm
- **They should not sleep after 5pm if you want them to go down well at 7pm.**
- Offer the first baby 20 minutes on the breast, then offer the second baby the breast for 20 minutes.
- **If they have been very awake during the day or didn't nap well between 4.30pm and 5pm, they may need to start their bath early.**

5.45pm
- Lay out things needed for bath and bedtime.
- Allow them both a good kick without their nappies while preparing the bath.

6pm

- The one who woke first at 2.15pm must start the bath no later than 6pm, and be massaged and dressed by 6.15pm.

6.15pm

- **The one bathed first must start his bottle feed no later than 6.15pm.**
- The second one must start his bath no later than 6.15pm, and be massaged and dressed by 6.30pm.

6.30pm

- **The second one must start his bottle feed no later than 6.30pm.**
- This should be done in the nursery with dim lights and no talking or eye contact.
- **Very important; they need to be in bed two hours from the time they last woke.**

7pm

- **They should both be fully swaddled and settled in the dark no later than 7pm.**

10.15pm

- Turn on the lights fully and unswaddle them so they wake up naturally. Allow at least ten minutes before feeding to ensure they are fully awake to feed well.
- Lay out things for their nappy change.

10.30pm

- Give them most of their bottle feed, change nappies and half swaddle (under the arms).
- **Dim the lights and with no talking or eye contact give remainder of feed.**
- This feed should take no more than one hour.

Routine for a breast-feeding baby at four to six weeks

Feed times	Nap times between 7am and 7pm
7am	9am–10am
10.30am	11.30/12 noon–2/2.30pm
2/2.30pm	4.15pm/5pm
5pm	
6.15pm	
10.30pm	**Maximum daily sleep 4½ hours**

Expressing times: 6.45am, 9.45am and 10pm

7am
- **Baby should be awake, nappy changed and feeding no later than 7am.**
- If he fed at 3am or 4am he needs 20–25 minutes on the full breast. If he's still hungry offer 10–15 minutes from the second breast after you have expressed 60–90ml (2–3oz).
- If he fed at 5am or 6am offer him 20–25 minutes from the second breast after expressing 60–90ml (2–3oz).
- **Do not feed after 7.45am, as it will put him off his next feed.** He can stay awake for up to two hours.

8am
- You should have cereal, toast and a drink no later than 8am.

8.45am
- Baby should start to get a bit sleepy by this time. **Even if he does not show the signs, he will be getting tired, so take him to his room now.**
- Check his nappy and draw sheet and close the curtains.

9am
- **When he is drowsy, settle baby, fully or half swaddled and in the dark with the door shut, no later than 9am.**

- He needs a sleep of no longer than one hour.
- Wash and sterilize bottles and expressing equipment.

9.45am
- Open the curtains and unswaddle baby so that he can wake up naturally.
- Prepare things for top-and-tailing and dressing.

10am
- **Baby must be fully awake now regardless of how long he slept.**
- Wash and dress him, remembering to cream all his creases and dry skin.

10.30am
- Baby should be given 20–25 minutes from the breast he last fed on.
- Lay him on his play mat so that he can have a good kick while you express 30ml (1oz) from the second breast. Then offer him 10–15 minutes.
- **Do not feed after 11.30am, as it will put him off his next feed.**

11.30am
- If baby was very alert and awake during the previous two hours, he may start to get tired by 11.30am and would need to be in bed by 11.45am.

11.45am
- Regardless of what he has done earlier, he should now be taken to his room.
- Check the draw sheet and change his nappy.
- Close the curtains and **when he is drowsy settle him, fully swaddled and in the dark with the door shut, no later than 12 noon.**

11.30/12 noon–2/2.30pm
- Baby needs a nap of no longer than two and a half hours from the time he went down.
- **If he wakes up after 45 minutes check the swaddle, but do not talk to him or turn the lights on.**

- Allow 20 minutes for him to resettle himself; if he is still unsettled offer him half the 2pm feed.
- Try to settle him back to sleep until 2.30pm.

12 noon
- Wash and sterilize expressing equipment and then have lunch and rest before the next feed.

2.20pm
- **Baby must be awake and feeding no later than 2.30pm regardless of how long he has slept.**
- Open the curtains, unswaddle him and allow him to wake up naturally. Change his nappy.
- Give 20–25 minutes from the breast he last fed on, then offer him 10–15 minutes from the other breast while you drink a large glass of water.
- **Do not feed after 3.15pm as it will put him off his next feed.**
- **It is very important that he is fully awake now until 4.15pm, so that he goes down well at 7pm;** if he was very alert in the morning he may be more sleepy now. Do not put too many clothes on him, as extra warmth will make him drowsy.
- Lay him on his play mat and encourage him to have a good kick.

4.15pm
- Change baby's nappy. This is a good time to take him for a walk to ensure that he sleeps well, and is refreshed for his bath and next feed. He may start to cut right back on this nap.
- **Baby should not sleep after 5pm if you want him to go down well at 7pm.**

5pm
- **Baby must be fully awake, and feeding no later than 5pm.**
- Give him a good 20 minutes on the breast he last fed on.
- **It is very important that baby is not allowed the other breast until after his bath.**

5.45pm
- If he has been very wakeful during the day or did not nap well between 4pm and 5pm, he may need to start his bath early.
- Allow him a good kick without his nappy while preparing things needed for his bath and bedtime.

6pm
- He must start his bath no later than 6pm, and be massaged and dressed by 6.15pm.

6.15pm
- He must be feeding no later than 6.15pm.
- This should be done in the nursery with dim lights and no talking or eye contact.
- If he did not empty the first breast at 5pm, allow 5–10 minutes on that one, before putting him on the full breast.
- Give him a good 20–25 minutes on the full breast while you drink a large glass of water.
- It is very important that he is in bed two hours from when he last awoke.

7pm
- Settle baby, fully or half swaddled (under the arms) and in the dark with the door shut, no later than 7pm.

8pm
- It is very important for you to have a really good meal and a rest before feeding or expressing at 10/10.30pm.

10/10.30pm
- Turn on the lights fully and unswaddle baby so that he can wake up naturally. Allow at least ten minutes before feeding to ensure that he is fully awake, so that he can feed well.
- Lay out things for the nappy change, plus a spare draw sheet, muslin and swaddle blanket in case they are needed in the middle of the night.
- Give him 20 minutes on the first breast or most of his bottle feed, change his nappy and re-swaddle him.

- Dim the lights and with no talking or eye contact give him 20 minutes on the second breast or the remainder of the bottle feed.
- This feed should take no longer than one hour.

In the night
- If he wakes up before 4am, give him a full feed.
- If he wakes up between 4am and 5am give one breast, then the second at 7am after expressing.
- If he wakes up at 6am give one breast, then the second at 7.30am after expressing.
- Always avoid eye contact and talking, and keep the lights low. Don't change his nappy unless absolutely necessary.

Changes to be made during the four- to six-week routine

His daily nap time between 7am and 7pm should be reduced to a strict four and a half hours: the morning nap should be no more than one hour, the lunch time nap no more than 30 minutes between 4.15pm and 5pm.

If your baby is very sleepy during the day and not managing to stay awake for the suggested times check Chapter 4 to see if this could become a real problem.

It is very important that by the end of six weeks you start to get your baby used to being half swaddled (under the arms) at the 9am and the 7pm sleeps. Cot death rates peak between two and four months and over-heating is considered to play a major factor in cot death.

It should now take less time to settle your baby to sleep. The cuddling time should gradually be reduced and now is a good time to get him used to going down when he is more awake. Often a lullaby light, which plays a tune and casts images on the ceiling for ten minutes or so, will help a baby to settle himself.

Your baby should start to sleep a longer stretch in the night around now, provided he is getting most of his daily milk intake between 6–7am and 11.30pm. A good indicator of this will be his weight gain; he should regularly be gaining 6–8oz each week. He would also need to be staying awake for nearer two hours at his social time.

Once he has done this stretch several nights in a row, try not to feed him if he suddenly goes back to waking earlier again. The hours after the 10.30pm feed are sometimes referred to as the 'core night' and if he wakes during these hours you could follow the 'core night method'. On waking at this time he should initially be left for a few minutes to settle himself back to sleep. If that doesn't work then other methods apart from feeding should be used to settle him. I would try settling him with some cool boiled water or a cuddle, others recommend a dummy. Attention should be kept to the minimum while reassuring the baby that you are there. This teaches the baby one of the most important sleep skills: how to go back to sleep after surfacing from a non-REM sleep. Obviously, if he refuses to settle you would need to feed him. This method could also be used to encourage an older baby who has got into the habit of waking at the same time in the night to sleep longer.

Before embarking on this method, the following points should be read carefully to make sure that your baby really is capable of going for a longer spell in the night:

- These methods should never be used with a very small baby or a baby who is not gaining weight. A baby not gaining weight should always be seen by a doctor.
- The above methods should only be used if your baby is regularly gaining 6–8oz each week, and if you are sure that his last feed is substantial enough to help him sleep for the longer stretch in the night.
- The main sign that a baby is ready to cut down on a night feed is regular weight gain and the reluctance to feed, or take less at the 7am feed.

The aim of this method is gradually to increase the length of time your baby can go from his last feed and not to eliminate the night feed in one go.

The core night method can be used if, over three or four nights, a baby has shown signs that he is capable of sleeping for a longer stretch.

Feeding

If your baby is feeding between 3am and 4am and you have to wake him up at 7am every morning, very gradually and by a very small amount, cut back the amount of milk he is taking in the night. This will have the knock-on effect of him drinking more during the day and less in the night, and eventually he will drop the middle-of-the-night feed altogether. It is important not to cut back too much or too fast as the baby could then start waking up long before 7am, which would defeat the whole purpose of getting him to sleep through to 7am from 11pm.

Increase the day feeds, not the night feeds. Cut back on the first expressing of the day by a further 30ml (1oz) and by the end of six weeks cut out the 10.30am expressing completely. Most babies are happy to wait longer after the 7am feed, so gradually keep pushing the 10am feed forward until 10.30am. The exception to this would be a baby who is getting to nearer 5am in the morning and having a top-up at 7.30am. It is unlikely that he would get through to 10.30am on having only a top-up feed at 7.30am, therefore continue to feed him at 10am until he is feeding between 6am and 7am.

Most babies go through a second growth spurt at six weeks, and want to spend longer on the breast at some feeds. Bottle-fed babies should have the 7am, the 10.30am and the 6.15pm feeds increased first during growth spurts. If during this growth spurt your baby's lunch-time nap becomes unsettled, it would be worthwhile giving him a small top-up prior to him going down for his nap. Once he has done a week of uninterrupted midday naps, gradually cut back on the top-up until you have eliminated it altogether.

Routine for a breast-feeding baby at six to eight weeks

Feed times	Nap times between 7am and 7pm
7am	9–9.45am
10.45am	11.45/12 noon–2/2.30pm
2/2.30pm	4.30–5pm
6.15pm	
10.30pm	**Maximum daily sleep 4 hours**
Expressing times: 6.45am and 10pm	

7am
- Baby should be awake, nappy changed and feeding no later than 7am.
- If he fed at 4am or 5am offer him 20–25 minutes on the full breast. If he's still hungry offer 10–15 minutes from the second breast after you have expressed 30–60ml (1–2oz).
- If he fed at 6am offer him 20–25 minutes from the second breast after you have expressed 30–60ml (1–2oz).
- Do not feed after 7.45am, as it will put him off his next feed. He can stay awake for up to two hours.

8am
- You should have cereal, toast and a drink no later than 8am.
- Wash and dress baby, remembering to cream all his creases and dry skin.

8.50am
- Check his nappy and draw sheet and close the curtains.

9am
- Settle the drowsy baby, half swaddled and in the dark with the door shut, no later than 9am.
- He needs a sleep of no longer than 45 minutes.
- Wash and sterilize bottles and expressing equipment.

9.45am
- Open the curtains and unswaddle baby so that he can wake up naturally.

10am

- Baby must be fully awake now, regardless of how long he slept.
- If he had a full feed at 7am he should last until 10.45am for his next feed. If he fed earlier followed by a top-up at 7.30am, he may need to start this 10am feed slightly earlier.
- Encourage him to have a good kick under his play gym.

10.45am

- He should be given 20–25 minutes from the breast he last fed on, then offered 10–15 minutes from the second breast while you have a large glass of water.
- Do not feed after 11.30am, as it will put him off his next feed.

11.45am

- Regardless of what he has done earlier, he should now be taken to his room.
- Check the draw sheet and change his nappy.
- Close the curtains and settle baby, half or fully swaddled and in the dark with the door shut, no later than 12 noon.

11.45/12 noon–2/2.30pm

- Baby needs a nap of no longer than two and a half hours from the time he went down.

12 noon

- Wash and sterilize bottles and expressing equipment, then have lunch and a rest before the next feed.

2.30pm

- Baby must be awake and feeding no later than 2.30pm, regardless of how long he has slept.
- Open the curtains, unswaddle him and allow him to wake up naturally. Change his nappy.
- Give 20–25 minutes from the breast he last fed on, then offer him 10–15 minutes from the other breast while you drink a large glass of water.
- Do not feed after 3.15pm as it will put him off his next feed.

- **It is very important that he is fully awake now until 4.30pm, so that he goes down well at 7pm.**
- If he was very alert in the morning he may be more sleepy now. Do not put too many clothes on him, as extra warmth will make him drowsy.
- Lay him on his play mat and encourage him to have a good kick.

4.15pm
- Change his nappy, and offer him a drink of cool boiled water or well-diluted juice no later than 4.30pm. (If, once your baby reaches eight weeks, he refuses water, try him with water with a hint of peach juice.)
- This is a good time to take him for a walk to ensure that he sleeps well, and is refreshed for his bath and next feed.

5pm
- **Baby must be fully awake now if you want him to go down well at 7pm.**
- If he is very hungry offer him 10–15 minutes on the breast he last fed on, otherwise try and get him to wait until after his bath for a full feed. By eight weeks he should be happy to wait until after the bath.

5.30pm
- Allow him a good kick without his nappy while preparing things needed for his bath and bedtime.

5.45pm
- He must start his bath no later than 5.45pm, and be massaged and dressed by 6.15pm.

6.15pm
- **He must be feeding no later than 6.15pm and this should be done in the nursery with dim lights and no talking or eye contact.**
- If he fed at 5pm, allow him a further 10–15 minutes to empty that breast completely, before putting him on the second breast.

- If he did not feed at 5pm, he should start on the breast he last fed on. Give him 20 minutes on each breast while you drink a large glass of water.
- It is very important that he is in bed two hours from when he last woke up.

7pm
- Settle baby, half swaddled and in the dark with the door shut, no later than 7pm.

8pm
- It is very important that you have a really good meal and a rest before the next feed or expressing.

10/10.30pm
- Turn on the lights fully and unswaddle baby so that he can wake up naturally. Allow at least ten minutes before feeding to ensure that he is fully awake, so that he can feed well.
- Lay out things for the nappy change, plus a spare draw sheet, muslin and swaddle blanket in case they are needed in the middle of the night.
- Give him 20 minutes on the first breast or most of his bottle feed, change his nappy and re-swaddle him.
- Dim the lights and with no talking or eye contact give him 20 minutes on the second breast or the remainder of the bottle feed.
- This feed should take no longer than one hour.

In the night
- If he is feeding before 4am, feeding well and losing interest in his 7am feed, it would be wise to try settling him with some cool boiled water. If he even takes an ounce or two before going on the breast, it should have the knock-on effect of him feeding better at 7am. The aim is to get him to take all his daily requirements between 7am and 11pm. If he is gaining 6–8oz of weight each week, it is important that he is encouraged to cut down and eventually drop the night feed.

- If he wakes between 4am and 5am give one breast, then the second at 7am after expressing.
- If he wakes up at 6am give one breast, then the second at 7.30am after expressing.
- As before, keep lights low and any stimulation to a minimum. No nappy change unless absolutely necessary.

Changes to be made during the six- to eight-week routine

Sleep

Most babies who weigh over 9lb should be sleeping longer in the night now, provided they are getting most of their daily nutritional needs between 6-7am and 11pm. They should also be sleeping no more than four hours between 7am and 7pm. Once he has lasted longer for several nights in a row, try not to feed your baby before that time again. The morning nap should be no more than 45 minutes, the lunch-time nap should be between $2^1/4$ and $2^1/2$ hours – no longer, and the afternoon nap should be no more than 30 minutes. He may catnap on and off during this nap; some babies cut out this nap altogether. Do not allow him to cut out this nap if he is not managing to stay awake until 7pm. If you want him to sleep until 7am, it is important that he goes to sleep nearer 7pm. If for some reason the lunch-time nap went wrong he may need slightly more sleep after the 2pm feed. Some babies will have a catnap after the 2pm feed at around 3pm of about 15 minutes, then a further catnap around 4.30–5pm.

He should now be half swaddled at the 9am and 7pm sleeps, and at 12 noon and from 11pm to 7am by the end of eight weeks. Some babies may start to wake up earlier in the night again once they are out of the swaddle; try and settle without feeding or re-swaddling.

Feeding

If your baby goes back to waking up earlier again, wait ten minutes or so before going to him. If he will not settle himself back to sleep, try settling him with some water or a cuddle.

Keep increasing day feeds, not night feeds. Most babies are happy to wait longer after the 7am feed, so keep pushing this feed forward until he is feeding at 10.45am. However, if your baby is still feeding at 5–6am with a top-up at 7–7.30am he may not manage to go longer and would need to have at least half of his next feed at 10am. Most babies go through a second growth spurt at six weeks. Cut back on the first expressing of the day by a further 30ml (1oz) and by the end of eight weeks cut out the 6.45am expressing so your baby gets the extra milk he needs. He may also need to spend longer on the breast at some feeds during growth spurts.

Bottle-fed babies should have the 7am, 10.45am and 6.15pm feeds increased first during growth spurts. The 10.30pm feed should only be increased if all the other feeds have been increased, and he is not going a longer spell in the night. Try not to give more then 180ml (6oz) at this feed. Some babies will need to move to a medium flow teat with three holes at this stage.

Routine for a breast-feeding baby at eight to twelve weeks

Feed times	Nap times between 7am and 7pm
7am	9–9.45am
10.45/11am	12 noon–2/2.15pm
2/2.15pm	4.45–5pm
6.15pm	
10.30pm	**Maximum daily sleep 3 1/2 hours**
Expressing at 10pm	

7am

- **Baby should be awake, nappy changed and feeding no later than 7am.**
- He should be given 20 minutes from the first breast, then offered 10–15 minutes from the second breast.
- **Do not feed after 7.45am, as it will put him off his next feed.**
- He can stay awake for up to two hours.

8am

- You should have cereal, toast and a drink no later than 8am.
- Wash and dress baby, remembering to cream all his creases and dry skin.

8.50am

- Check his nappy and draw sheet and close the curtains.

9am

- **Settle the drowsy baby, half swaddled and in the dark with the door shut, no later than 9am.**
- He needs a sleep of no longer than 45 minutes.
- Wash and sterilize bottles and expressing equipment.

9.45am

- Open the curtains and unswaddle baby so that he can wake up naturally.

10am

- Baby must be fully awake now, regardless of how long he slept.
- Encourage him to have a good kick under his play gym.

10.45/11am

- He should be given 20 minutes from the breast he last fed on, then offered 10–15 minutes from the second breast while you have a large glass of water.
- **Do not feed after 11.30am, as it will put him off his next feed.**

11.55am
- Regardless of what he has done earlier, he should now be taken to his room.
- Check the draw sheet and change his nappy.
- Close the curtains and **settle baby, half swaddled and in the dark with the door shut, no later than 12 noon.**

12 noon–2/2.15pm
- Baby needs a nap of no longer than $2^1/4$ hours from the time he went down.
- Wash and sterilize bottles and expressing equipment.

2/2.15pm
- **Baby must be awake $2^1/4$ hours from the time he went down, regardless of how he has slept, and he must be feeding no later than 2.30pm.**
- Open the curtains, unswaddle him and allow him to wake up naturally. Change his nappy.
- Give 20 minutes from the breast he last fed on, then offer him 10–15 minutes from the other breast while you drink a large glass of water.
- **Do not feed after 3.15pm as it will put him off his next feed.**
- **It is very important that he is fully awake now until 4.45pm, so that he goes down well at 7pm.**

4.15pm
- Change his nappy, and offer him a drink of cool boiled water or well-diluted juice no later than 4.30pm.
- He may have a short nap between 4.45pm and 5pm.

5pm
- **Baby must be fully awake if you want him to sleep at 7pm.**
- He should be happy to wait until after the bath for his feed.

5.30pm
- Allow him a good kick without his nappy while preparing things needed for his bath and bedtime.

5.45pm
- He must start his bath no later than 5.45pm, and be massaged and dressed by 6.15pm.

6.15pm
- He must be feeding no later than 6.15pm and this should be done in the nursery with dim lights and no talking or eye contact.
- He should be given 20 minutes on each breast while you drink a large glass of water.
- It is very important that he is in bed two hours from when he last awoke.

7pm
- Settle the drowsy baby, half swaddled and in the dark with the door shut, no later than 7pm.

8pm
- It is very important that you have a really good meal and a rest before the next feed or expressing.

10/10.30pm
- Turn on the lights fully and unswaddle baby so that he can wake up naturally. Allow at least ten minutes before feeding to ensure that he is fully awake, so that he can feed well.
- Lay out things for the nappy change, plus a spare draw sheet, muslin and swaddle blanket in case they are needed in the middle of the night.
- Give him 20 minutes on the first breast or most of his bottle feed, change his nappy and re-swaddle him.
- Dim the lights and with no talking or eye contact give him 20 minutes on the second breast or the remainder of the bottle feed.
- This feed should take no longer than one hour.

In the night
- If your baby is feeding before 5am, feeding well and losing interest in his 7am feed, it would be wise to try settling him

with some cool boiled water. Remember, the aim is to get him to take all his daily requirements between 7am and 11pm. As long as he is gaining 6oz a week, he can be encouraged to go through to 5am without a milk feed.

- If he wakes up at 5am give him the first breast, and if needed 5–10 minutes on the second breast.
- If he wakes up at 6am give the first breast, then the second at 7.30am.
- Avoid night-time stimulation; only change his nappy if necessary.

Changes to be made during the eight- to twelve-week routine

Sleep

Most babies who weigh nearer 12lb in weight can manage to go through the night from the 10–11pm feed at this age, provided they are taking all their daily nutritional needs between 7am and 11pm. They should also be sleeping no more than three and a half hours between 7am and 7pm. A totally breast fed baby may still be waking up once in the night, hopefully nearer 5am or 6am.

Cut back your baby's daily nap time by a further 30 minutes, to a total of three hours. The morning nap should be no more than 45 minutes, but if he is not sleeping so well at lunchtime, it can be cut back to 30 minutes. The lunchtime nap should be no more than two and a quarter hours. It is around this stage that the lunchtime nap can sometimes go wrong. The baby comes into a light sleep usually 30–45 minutes after he has gone to sleep. Some babies will wake up fully and it is important that they learn how to settle themselves back to sleep if the wrong sleep associations are to be avoided. For more details on this problem refer to Chapter 4.

Most babies have cut out their late afternoon nap, but if this is not so, do not allow more than 15 minutes, unless for some reason the lunch-time nap has gone wrong and then it would be slightly longer. All babies should only be half swaddled and sleeping in their big cots; particular attention should be paid when tucking the baby in the cot.

One reason many babies of this age still wake up is because they move around the cot and get their arms and legs caught in between the spars. If this is happening with your baby I would advise that you purchase one of the very light summer-weight sleeping bags from the company named at the back of the book. They are so lightweight that you can still use a sheet and one blanket to tuck them in, without the worry of overheating.

(See pages 3–6 for further details on cots and bedding.)

Feeding

Your baby should be well established on five feeds a day now, eventually taking a very small feed at 10pm. If he is totally breast fed and has started waking up earlier in the morning, it may be worth trying a top-up from a bottle of either expressed or formula milk after you feed him at 10pm. If he is sleeping regularly to 7am, gradually bring the 10.30–11pm feed forward by five minutes every three nights until he is feeding at 10pm. As long as he continues to sleep through to 7am and takes a full feed, then you can keep taking the 10.45am feed back until he is feeding at 11am.

If you are considering introducing a further bottle-feed the best time to introduce it is at the 11am feed. Gradually reduce the time of the feed by two or three minutes each day and top up with formula. By the end of the first week, if your baby is taking a bottle-feed of 150–180ml (5–6oz), you should be able to drop the breast feed easily without the risk of serious engorgement. Bottle-fed babies should continue to have their 7am, 11am and 6.15pm feeds increased first during the next growth spurt at around nine weeks. Increase the bottle-feed to suit your baby's needs.

Routine for a baby at three to four months

Feed times	Nap times between 7am and 7pm
7am	9–9.45am
11am	12 noon–2/2.15pm
2.15/2.30pm	
6.15pm	
10.30pm	**Maximum daily sleep 3 hours**

7am
- **Baby should be awake, nappy changed and feeding no later than 7am.**
- He should feed from both breasts or take a full bottle feed and then should stay awake for two hours.

8am
- He should be encouraged to have a kick on his play mat for 20–30 minutes.
- Wash and dress baby, remembering to cream all his creases and dry skin.

9am
- **Settle the drowsy baby, half swaddled and in the dark with the door shut no later than 9am.** He needs a sleep of no longer than 45 minutes.
- Wash and sterilize bottles and expressing equipment.

9.45am
- Open the curtains and unswaddle him so that he can wake up naturally.

10am
- **Baby must be fully awake now regardless of how long he slept.**
- Encourage him to have a good kick under his play gym.

11am
- He should be given a feed from both breasts or a full bottle feed.
- Do not feed after 11.30am as it will put him off his next feed.

11.50am
- Check the draw sheet and change his nappy.
- Close the curtains and **settle the drowsy baby, half swaddled and in the dark with the door shut, no later than 12 noon.**

12 noon–2/2.15pm
- Baby needs a nap of no longer than two and a quarter hours from the time he went down. Wash and sterilize bottles and expressing equipment.

2/2.15pm
- **Baby must be awake two and a quarter hours from the time he was put to bed, regardless of how long he has slept, and he must be feeding no later than 2.30pm.**
- Open the curtains, unswaddle him and allow him to wake naturally, then change his nappy.
- He needs a feed from both breasts or a bottle feed.
- **Do not feed him after 3.15pm as it will put him off his next feed.**
- If he has slept well at both naps he should manage to get through the rest of the afternoon without a further sleep.

4.15pm
- Change his nappy and offer him a drink of cool boiled water or well-diluted juice no later than 4.30pm.

5.30pm
- Put him on the changing mat on the floor without his nappy, so that he can have a good kick while you prepare his bath.

5.45pm
- Baby must start his bath no later than 5.45pm, and be massaged and dressed no later than 6.15pm.

6.15pm
- He must be feeding no later than 6.15pm.
- He should feed from both breasts or have 210–240ml (7–8oz) of formula milk.
- Dim the lights and sit him in his chair for ten minutes while you tidy up.

7pm
- Settle the drowsy baby, half swaddled and in the dark with the door shut, no later than 7pm.

10.30pm
- Turn the lights on low and wake him enough to feed.
- Give him most of his breast feed or 180ml (6oz) bottle feed, change his nappy and half swaddle him.
- Dim the lights and with no talking or eye contact give him the remainder of his feed. If he does not want the remainder do not force it, as he should start to cut back on this feed now.
- This feed should take no longer than 30 minutes.

Changes to be made during the three- to four-month routine

Sleeping

If you have structured the milk feeds and nap times according to the routine, your baby should manage to sleep through the night from his last feed to nearer 6–7am in the morning. If he shows signs of starting to wake up earlier it would be advisable to assume that it may be hunger and increase his 10pm feed. You should also ensure that his maximum daily sleep between 7am and 7pm totals no more than three hours. Most babies will cut right back on their late afternoon sleep and some days may manage to get through the afternoon without the nap, but may need to go to bed 5–10 minutes earlier.

If for some reason your baby slept less than two hours at lunch-time he should certainly be encouraged to have a short nap between 4 and 5pm, otherwise he may become so over-tired at bedtime that he doesn't settle to sleep easily.

The time your baby is awake at the 10.30pm feed should be gradually reduced to 30 minutes, provided he is sleeping through regularly to 7am. If he is still waking up between 5 and 6am it would be advisable to try and keep him awake for at least an hour at the last feed.

Even if he is not getting out of his half swaddle I would suggest that now is a good time to get him used to a 100 per cent **cotton** very lightweight sleeping bag. He would still need to be tucked in firmly, therefore it is important that you purchase a 0.5 tog bag to avoid the risk of overheating.

Feeding

A formula-fed baby who is taking 1050–1200ml (35–40oz) of formula between 7am and 11pm should not really need to feed in the night. However, some very big babies who weigh over 15lb at this stage may still need to feed between 5am and 6am, followed by a top-up at 7–7.30am until he reaches four months and is weaned. I would not advise that a baby is weaned before four months unless advised by a paediatrician.

It is better to keep feeding in the night for a slightly longer time than take the risk of your baby developing allergies. A totally breast-fed baby may also need to feed around 5–6am as he may not be getting enough to eat at the last feed. Regardless of whether he is breast or bottle fed, a good indicator of whether a baby is ready to drop the night feed is how he takes his top-up at 7–7.30am. If he takes it greedily then he is probably genuinely hungry at 5–6am. If he fusses and frets and refuses the top-up I would assume the early wake-up was more habit than hunger and try to settle him back with some cool boiled water or a cuddle.

If your baby continues to sleep through to 7am once his waking time at 10.30pm has been reduced to 30 minutes, plus he is cutting back on his 7am feed, start reducing the amount he is drinking at 10–10.30pm. Only continue with this if he is sleeping well until 7am. Once he is taking 60ml (2oz) at the last feed and sleeps through consecutively for seven nights, drop this feed.

Robert: aged four months

Robert was being totally breast fed apart from one feed of formula when his mother contacted me. She was very concerned that despite introducing solids he still was demanding to be fed two-hourly, day and night. He seemed to have none of the usual association problems and he would, when ready to sleep, go down in his cot happily without needing to be rocked, patted or fed.

When he did wake in the night he would feed quickly and go straight back to sleep. The only real problem was that he needed to be fed every two hours.

He went from a weight of just over 8lb at birth to 16lb at four months. This was an excellent weight gain, and certainly proved he was getting enough to eat. I suggested that his mother should continue to give Robert the baby rice, but introduce it after the 6pm feed instead of the 2.30pm one. The one bottle feed should be moved to 10.30pm, instead of 10.30am. For the rest of his milk feeds and his sleep, I advised her to put him on the six-week routine. If he adapted to that routine well, she should gradually move him through the routines until he was on the one suitable for his age.

By the end of two weeks Robert was happily established in the four-month routine, and sleeping through most nights from the 10.30pm feed to 7am. Unfortunately Robert's parents had only enjoyed a week of him sleeping through regularly to 7am, when he developed a cold. He continued to feed well, his routine during the day was fine and he also settled well at 7pm, but like most young babies who develop a cold he became very unsettled in the middle of the night. His parents propped up his cot and used a vaporizor, but the mucus in Robert's nose caused him so much distress that the only way his mother could keep him calm was to put him upright on her chest. The cold lingered on for nearly two weeks, and by the time he was completely clear of the cold he was so used to waking up at 3am, that he continued to do so. The mother was exhausted by this time, and so ended up giving him a dummy at the 3am waking. As I predicted, he started to look for it during other sleeps.

By the time he reached six months all his naps had gone wrong, he was difficult to settle at 7pm and would wake up regularly in the night. I suggested sleep training, but the mother felt sure he would eventually break the pattern. At the end of seven months she decided to take the dummy away completely, as things were so out of hand, and within a couple of nights of leaving him to cry for 20–30 minutes he had learned to settle himself. However, he did continue to wake up at least once in the middle of the night, but the parents usually got him back to sleep by stroking his forehead.

The mother was returning to work when Robert was nine months old, and she realized that with her demanding job she would not be able to cope if he continued to wake up even once a night. The parents by this time had spoken to several other couples who had done sleep training, and decided it was now or never. **Unfortunately** for them and the baby they did not adhere to the golden rule when sleep training a baby, which is never to pick the baby up when he is crying. They would let him cry for 30–50 minutes, and become so overwhelmed with guilt that they would then pick him up and rock him to sleep, even though I had told them repeatedly that sleep training should only be done if the parents feel they are disciplined enough to carry it through. By picking the baby up after 40 minutes of crying they were actually teaching him that if he cried long enough he would get picked up. Even worse, because he was so exhausted from being awake in the night, he became very unhappy and irritable during the daytime.

The mother, now back at work, became so exhausted trying to cope with work and getting up in the night, that she decided to give sleep training one last try. I put her in contact with several mothers who had gone through a similar situation, in the hope that this would give her confidence to follow the sleep training properly. The first night Robert cried for over three hours; the parents did not go in at all. They lay in bed holding hands and crying themselves, and vowing never to let it get to this stage if they had a second baby. The second night he cried again for three hours; but this time there were longer intervals between the crying. On the third night he slept through from 7.30pm to 7am, and continued to sleep well for many months until he caught another cold. This time when he was over the cold, they immediately left him to settle himself, which only took a couple of nights of very little crying.

The majority of babies will automatically go back into the routine the minute they recover from an illness, but a few, like Robert, do have to be sleep trained.

Routine for a baby at four to five months

Feed times	Nap times between 7am and 7pm
7am	9–9.45am
11am	12 noon–2/2.15pm
2.30pm	
6pm	
10pm	**Maximum daily sleep 3 hours**

7am
- Baby should be awake, nappy changed and feeding no later than 7am.
- He should feed from both breasts or have a full bottle feed.
- He should stay awake for two hours.

8am
- He should be encouraged to have a kick on his play mat for 20 30 minutes.
- Wash and dress baby, remembering to cream all his creases and dry skin.

9am
- Settle the drowsy baby, half swaddled and in the dark with the door shut no later than 9am. He needs a sleep of no longer than 45 minutes.
- Wash and sterilize bottles and expressing equipment.

9.45am
- Open the curtains and unswaddle him so that he can wake up naturally.

10am
- **Baby must be fully awake now regardless of how long he slept.** Encourage him to have a good kick under his play gym or take him on an outing.

11am
- He should be given a full breast feed or a full bottle feed, before being offered a small amount of puréed vegetables.
- Encourage him to sit in his chair while you clear away the lunch things.

11.50am
- Check the draw sheet and change his nappy.
- Close the curtains and **settle the drowsy baby, half swaddled in the dark with the door shut no later than 12 noon.**

12 noon–2/2.15pm
- **He will need a nap now of no longer than two and a quarter hours from the time he went down.** Wash and sterilize bottles and expressing equipment.

2.15pm/2.30pm
- **Baby must be awake two and a quarter hours from the time he went down, regardless of how long he has slept, and he must be feeding no later than 2.30pm.**
- Open the curtains, unswaddle him and allow him to wake up naturally. Change his nappy.
- He needs a feed from both breasts or a full bottle feed.
- **Do not feed him after 3.15pm as it will put him off his next feed.**
- If he has slept well at both naps he may manage to get through the rest of the afternoon without a further sleep.

4.15pm
- Change baby's nappy, and offer him a drink of cool boiled water or well-diluted juice no later than 4.30pm.

5.15pm
- Put him on the changing mat on the floor without his nappy, so that he can have a good kick while you prepare the bath.

5.30pm
- He must start his bath no later than 5.35pm, and be massaged and dressed no later than 6pm.

6pm
- He must be feeding no later than 6pm.
- He should feed from both breasts or have a full bottle feed, before having the rice and fruit purée.
- Then dim the lights and sit him in his chair for ten minutes while you tidy up.

7pm
- Settle the drowsy baby, half swaddled and in the dark with the door shut, no later than 7pm.

10pm
- Turn the lights on low and wake him enough to feed.
- Give him most of his breast or bottle feed, change his nappy and half swaddle him.
- Dim the lights and with no talking or eye contact give him the remainder of the feed. If he does not want the remainder do not force it, as he should start to cut back on this feed now.
- This feed should take no longer than 30 minutes.

Changes to be made during the four- to five-month routine

Sleep

By the end of five months your baby should be sleeping from 7pm to 7am. If you have not already introduced a light-weight sleeping bag it would be advisable to do so at this stage. To leave it any later you may risk the problem of your baby being unhappy when he is put into it. It is very important that he is also still tucked in well. In very hot weather he can be put into his bag with just a nappy on and a very thin cotton sheet tucked lengthways across the width of the cot, with two rolled up towels wedged between the mattress and the spars of the cot to keep the sheet firm. If he is not sleeping well at lunch-time, cut back his morning nap to 20–30 minutes.

Feeding

When solids are introduced at four months, it is important that your baby still has most of his milk feed first. If you find that your baby is getting too tired to have milk at 6pm followed by the solids, then give him two-thirds of his milk at 5.40pm, followed by the solids. The bath time can then be moved to 6.30pm followed by the remainder of his milk at 6.45pm. Once solids are introduced at this feed he should automatically begin to cut back on his last feed.

If you have not already done so, start bringing the 10.30pm feed forward to 10pm, gradually reducing the amount as he increases his solids. By five months this feed should be dropped and he should be on four milk feeds between 7am and 7pm, and enjoying a varied selection of vegetables and fruit from the first stage weaning foods (see page 192).

Routine for a baby at five to six months

Feed times	Nap times between 7am and 7pm
7am	9–9.45am
11.30am	12.15–2/2.15pm
2.30pm	
6pm	**Maximum daily sleep 3 hours**

7am
- Baby should be awake, nappy changed and feeding no later than 7am.
- He should feed from both breasts or have a full bottle feed, followed by a small amount of breakfast cereal mixed with either expressed milk or formula.
- He should stay awake for two hours.

8am
- He should be encouraged to have a kick on his play mat for 20–30 minutes.
- Wash and dress baby, remembering to cream all his creases and dry skin.

9am
- Settle the drowsy baby, half swaddled and in the dark with the door shut, no later than 9am.
- He needs a sleep of no longer than 45 minutes.

9.45am
- Open the curtains and unswaddle him so that he can wake up naturally.

10am
- Baby must be fully awake now regardless of how long he slept.
- Encourage him to have a good kick under his play gym or take him on an outing.

11.30am
- He should be given half the milk feed followed by a selection of puréed vegetables, then offered the rest of the milk feed.
- Encourage him to sit in his chair while you clear away the lunch things.

12.10pm
- Check the draw sheet and change his nappy.
- Close the curtains and settle the drowsy baby, half swaddled and in the dark with the door shut, no later than 12.15pm.

12.15pm–2/2.15pm
- He will need a nap now of no longer than two hours from the time he went down.
- Wash and sterilize bottles and expressing equipment.

2.15pm
- Baby must be awake and feeding no later than 2.30pm regardless of how long he has slept.
- Open the curtains, unswaddle him and allow him to wake up naturally. Change his nappy.
- He needs a feed from both breasts or a full bottle feed.
- Do not feed him after 3.15pm as it will put him off his next feed.

4.15pm
- Change baby's nappy, and offer him a drink of cool boiled water or well-diluted juice no later than 4.30pm.

5.15pm
- Put him on the changing mat on the floor without his nappy, so he can have a good kick while you prepare the bath.

5.30pm
- He must start his bath no later than 5.30pm, and be massaged and dressed no later than 6pm.

6pm
- Baby must be feeding no later than 6pm.
- He should feed from both breasts or have a full bottle feed, before having the rice and fruit purée.
- Dim the lights and sit him in his chair for ten minutes while you tidy up.

7pm
- Baby should be half swaddled and settled in the dark with the door shut no later than 7pm.

Changes to be made during the five- to six-month routine

Sleep

Your baby should continue to sleep well between 7pm and 7am, provided he is taking four full milk feeds a day and not sleeping more than three hours between 7am and 7pm. Until he is able to crawl and manoeuvre himself around the cot, he still needs to be tucked in firmly.

The lunchtime naps should be pushed to 12.15pm to fit in with a later lunch. If he is not sleeping the full two hours at lunchtime, cut back his morning nap to 20–30 minutes.

Feeding

Once solids are established at 11am and 6pm, introduce breakfast cereal after the 7am milk feed, continuing to give all his milk first. When breakfast is well established you will probably find that you can gradually push to nearer 11.30am. It is very important that you start to use the tier system of feeding at this stage; this is where you alternate between milk and solids during a feed. By the time he reaches six months he should be taking more solids than milk at 11.30am. This will prepare him for dropping this milk feed altogether and replacing it with a cup of cool boiled water or well-diluted juice, once protein is introduced at six months.

James: aged 5¹/₂ months

James was 5¹/₂ months when his mother first called me, as she and his father were mentally and physically exhausted. James was settling well at 7pm, but woke up several times a night, sometimes staying awake for two hours at a time. No amount of feeding, rocking or walking the floor would pacify him. He was drinking well in excess of 1440ml (48oz) of formula milk a day, refusing solids, and never slept a wink between 7am and 7pm.

This was a particularly unusual case for me to try and solve. Normally I find that one of the main causes of repeated night wakings with babies over three months of age, is that they are having too much sleep between 7am and 7pm. This was not the case with James, and what a challenge he turned out to be! I observed him for the first 24 hours before deciding what plan of action to take. Unbelievably, he did not shut his eyes the whole day, and even more surprisingly he did not get hysterically overtired like babies of his age normally would if they had gone long spells without sleep. However, he did need constant attention and entertainment, which was absolutely exhausting for the poor mother, who had also been awake most of the night.

James would drink easily a 240ml (8oz) bottle of formula, but go berserk every time he was offered a spoonful of solids. I suggested that at 6pm we should try giving him only half of the formula, then offer the solids, but the same thing happened: he went berserk again. He would not stop screaming until we allowed him to finish the full 240ml (8oz) formula feed. We then proceeded to bath and settle him for the night and he went to sleep like a dream at 7pm, just as his mother said he would. At 10.30pm I woke him up for his last feed, when he drank 210ml (7oz) quickly, burped well and settled quickly back to sleep.

That night the parents each took a sleeping tablet plus a glass of red wine, and moved up to the top floor to get some much needed sleep. With James 'sleeping like a baby' in the room next to mine I was fast coming to the conclusion that the only real problem with James was that he was a milk-aholic and had very neurotic parents. I was convinced that with my expert handling the problem of night-time waking would be quickly solved! At 1am the screaming started, but refusing to believe that he could be hungry, I tried to settle him with a cuddle and some cool boiled water. It took me nearly 40 minutes to get him back to sleep, only to be awoken by the most horrendous screaming, an hour and a half later. This time he would not be pacified with water and a cuddle but kicked and screamed so much I thought he was going to go into a fit. All my logic went out of the window; I thought it must be hunger and offered him a full 240ml (8oz) bottle, which he quickly drank. I changed his nappy and settled him back in his cot, where he gurgled and talked to himself for another 30 minutes before going to sleep at 4am. He awoke again at 5am, one hour later. I now decided to get tough and use the controlled crying method. I went in every ten minutes to reassure him, but it was an hour and ten minutes before he eventually fell asleep at 6.10am. He then awoke on the dot of 7am in the happiest of moods, despite having been awake for nearly three hours in the night. The thought of trying to keep him entertained during the 12-hour day ahead, with no sleep for either him or me, filled me with horror. I very quickly decided the parents were not neurotic, but saints for having coped with him this far.

That day I decided that although he showed no signs of ever wanting to sleep during the day, I would try my routine for a five- to six-month baby. I put him down in the morning at 9am and he screamed for 25 minutes before dropping off to sleep. I then had to wake him at 10am. I put him back down at 12 noon and again he screamed for nearly 25 minutes, going to sleep at 12.25pm and waking up screaming 45 minutes later when he came into his light sleep. He screamed on and off for a further 45 minutes before falling asleep at 2pm. Although it was very tempting to let him sleep past 2.30pm, I know from past experience how important it was not to let a baby sleep past the feeding time, as the structuring of feeds in the early months plays a very important part in babies' sleep cycles. He stayed awake until 4.45pm, at which time he had a 15-minute nap in the buggy while out for a walk. We followed the same bath-time ritual and he went down well at 7pm, and like the previous night I fed him at 10.30pm, after which he settled well and went straight back to sleep.

He woke around 1am, and I decided to keep going with the controlled crying method, as the first waking in the night was due to habit more than hunger. I went in every 15–20 minutes to reassure him and again like the previous night it took about 45 minutes to settle him.

He then woke up again at 3am and this time it took around 30 minutes to settle him. When he woke for the third time at 5am, I felt that having gone over six hours for the first time ever without a feed he might be hungry, so I fed him. He took 210ml (7oz) quickly, but did not settle until 6.15am, and then woke up on the dot of 7am. The days and nights that followed formed much the same pattern for a further week, showing no real sign of improvement. I was beginning to feel pretty desperate, and the parents were even more desperate. The method of sleep training that had worked for so many other babies was not working here so I suggested to his mother that we should try not going in to him at all when he started crying, unless he got into difficulties.

He woke up on the dot of 1am, and went berserk; for over an hour he never gave up once. Eventually he went quiet, only to start yelling again an hour later. This went on and off until 5am, when he went quiet, and this time he did not wake at 7am. I got him up anyway, to try and keep him on track with his daytime sleep. That day saw a vast improvement; he only complained for a few minutes when going down for his naps, and at lunch-time woke up only briefly and settled himself back. That night we agreed to take the same approach: I would only go to him if he got into serious difficulties. He woke twice for approximately 40 minutes each time, but would settle himself back to sleep. For the next three days I stuck rigidly to his daytime routine and did not go to him at all when he woke up during his naps or night-time sleep. Each day and night the yelling got less and less, and by the fourth night, he fed at 11pm and slept straight through until 7am.

Having conquered the sleeping, James's mother asked me if I would stay on a further week to try and sort out his feeding. I have to admit I was none too keen, as he was such a demanding baby. But deep down I knew that if the problem of his refusing solids was not sorted out, his sleeping would eventually backtrack again. I agreed to stay for a further week, but on the condition that I did not have to entertain him every waking hour.

By not feeding James milk in the night, I had reduced his daily milk intake to 1140ml (38oz). But I realized that to get him interested in solids I would have to reduce it even further, to around 960ml (32oz). I did not want to cut back on his 10.30pm feed just yet, for fear he would wake up in the night again, so I decided to reduce the 2.30pm feed to 120ml (4oz). He was so hungry by the 6pm feed, that he drank 240ml (8oz) within ten minutes and took a small amount of baby rice mixed with a further 30ml (1oz) of formula. Normally I would start to introduce baby rice at the 11am feed, but because I felt James would have to be really hungry to accept solids, I continued increasing the baby rice at the 6pm feed.

Within four to five days of gradually increasing the amount of baby rice plus some pear purée at the 6pm feed, he started to cut right back on his 10.30pm feed. By the end of the week he was drinking only 60ml (2oz) of formula at that feed, and still sleeping through to 7am, so I felt confident that we could drop the 10.30pm feed. Dropping it would also have the knock-on effect of increasing his appetite during the day, allowing me to introduce some puréed vegetables after the 11am bottle feed.

During the final week I spent hours upon hours cooking and puréeing over 80lb of fruit and vegetables, optimistic that James would eventually grow to love his food. It was also a perfect way of keeping myself so busy that I did not have time to pick James up every time he yelled. With a little help from Madonna and Mozart he learned to kick and roll and play happily on the floor.

Years later, his mother informs me what a happy, contented little boy he is, who sleeps well and enjoys a very healthy, varied diet. Those very traumatic first six months could have been avoided altogether, if the innocent mother had not been misguided by her young maternity nurse. She advised that demand feeding was best, and that a baby should be allowed to find its own sleep pattern.

Routine for a baby at six to nine months

Feed times	Nap times between 7am and 7pm
7am	9–9.30/45am
11.45am	12.30–2.30pm
2.30pm	
5pm	
6.30pm	**Maximum daily sleep 3 hours**

7am
- Baby should be awake, nappy changed and feeding no later than 7am.
- He should feed from both breasts or have a full bottle feed, followed by breakfast cereal mixed with either expressed milk or formula and fruit.
- He should stay awake for two hours.

8am
- He should be encouraged to have a kick on his play mat for 20–30 minutes.
- Wash and dress baby, remembering to cream all his creases and dry skin.

9am
- Settle the drowsy baby, in his sleeping bag (see page 164) in the dark with the door shut and no later than 9am.
- He needs a sleep of 30–45 minutes.

9.30/9.45am
- Open the curtains and undo his sleeping bag so that he can wake up naturally.

10am
- Baby must be fully awake now regardless of how long he slept.
- Encourage him to have a good kick under his play gym or take him on an outing.

11.45am
- He should be given most of his solids before being offered a drink of water or well-diluted juice from a cup, then alternate between solids and a drink.
- Encourage him to sit in his chair while you clear away the lunch things.

12.20pm
- Check the draw sheet and change his nappy.
- Close the curtains and settle the drowsy baby, in his sleeping bag in the dark with the door shut and no later than 12.30pm.

12.30–2.30pm
- He will need a nap now of no longer than two hours from the time he went down.
- If he slept the full 45 minutes earlier, he may need less sleep at this nap.

2.30pm
- Baby must be awake and feeding no later than 2.30pm, regardless of how long he has slept.
- Open the curtains, and allow him to wake up naturally. Change his nappy.
- He needs a feed from both breasts or a full bottle feed.
- Do not feed him after 3.15pm as it will put him off his next feed.

4.15pm
- Change baby's nappy, and offer him a drink of cool boiled water or well-diluted juice no later than 4.30pm.

5pm
- He should be given most of his solids before being offered a small drink of water from a cup. It is important that he still has a good milk feed at bedtime, so keep this drink to a minimum.

6pm
- He must start his bath no later than 6pm and be massaged and dressed no later than 6.30pm.

6.30pm
- Baby must be feeding no later than 6.30pm. He should feed from both breasts or have 210ml (7oz) of formula feed.
- Dim the lights and sit him in his chair for ten minutes while you tidy up.

7pm
- Settle baby in his cot and in the dark with the door shut, no later than 7pm.

Changes to be made during the six- to nine-month routine

Sleep

Some babies are happy to sleep later in the morning once they are established on three solid meals a day. If your baby sleeps until nearer 8am in the morning he will not need a morning nap, but he may not manage to get through until 12.30pm for his lunch-time nap, therefore he may need to have lunch around 11.30am so he can go down at 12.15pm for his lunch-time nap.

Babies who continue to wake up at 7am may still need to go down for a short nap in the morning. This may be slightly later than 9am, but no later than 9.30am.

He may also start to roll on to his front and prefer to sleep on his tummy. When this happens it would be advisable to remove the sheet and blankets so as to avoid him getting into a tangle with them. In the winter months the lightweight sleeping bag will need to be replaced with a warmer one to make up for the loss of blankets.

Feeding

Continue to use the tier system of feeding at lunchtime. Once your baby is only taking a couple of ounces of milk at lunchtime, replace it with a drink of water or well-diluted juice from a cup. It is important that this is done once your baby is eating protein at lunchtime. Once the lunchtime milk is dropped he may need to increase the 2.30pm feed. However, if you notice that he is cutting back too much on his last feed, continue to keep this feed smaller.

At six months, his suppertime solids should be transferred and changed to a proper tea at 5pm, with only a small drink of water from a cup. He would then have a full milk feed around 6.30pm.

By nine months, bottle fed babies should be drinking all of their water, diluted juice and most of their milk feeds from a cup.

Eliza and Emily: aged six months

These twin girls suffered from severe eczema and their cheeks were so raw that at times they would bleed. It was so bad that it actually looked as if they had been burned with a hot iron. The mother also suffered from severe eczema and was desperate to minimize the pain she knew it could cause, so for six months she exclusively breast fed both babies, in the hope that it would help.

When the babies were weaned onto solids she sought the best possible advice from leading nutritionists and dermatologists. By the time she contacted me she was so physically and mentally exhausted from breast feeding on demand night and day, that she decided to give it up. I supported her decision totally as the eczema was so bad that formula milk could not make it any worse. Also, realistically, I do not think any human being could continue to survive on the small amount of sleep she and her husband were getting. However, there was a major problem: both babies simply refused to feed from a bottle.

I knew from past experience that this could be a very difficult problem to solve. The one thing in our favour was the babies' age, as they were both old enough to last a reasonable period of time without a breast feed. I agreed to move into their very small one-bedroom flat on the condition that their mother did not allow either baby on the breast from 11am that day. I arrived at 6pm in the evening and both babies were screaming the place down with hunger, as they had been used to feeding every two to three hours. Their mother had followed my instructions and not fed the babies, and we proceeded to attempt to feed them with expressed milk from a bottle. Eliza fought the bottle, but we did manage to get her to drink a small amount of milk. Emily screamed and fought the bottle so much that she drank nothing. I realized that I had a very tough night ahead of me, so I suggested to their mother that we allow Eliza the remainder of her milk feed from the breast. Hopefully she would settle for a few hours, allowing me to concentrate on Emily, whom I figured was going to be the bigger challenge.

We settled both babies in bed by 7pm, and went through what their mother had been weaning the babies on. The advice she had received from the dietitian was excellent; my only criticism was that there was no structure to the milk feeds.

This, in addition to the irritation of the eczema, was the main reason the babies were waking up. I was convinced that their exhausted mother could not to be producing enough milk for them both to get through the night.

Eliza slept through until 3am, at which time with a bit of a struggle I managed to get her to drink 90ml (3oz) of formula. She settled back to sleep until 6.30am. Emily was much more difficult because she had not had a proper milk feed since 2pm, and so was very unsettled the whole night. I was concerned that she should not become dehydrated, so I resorted to spooning milk into her whenever she woke up, which was roughly every hour. By 5am the following morning she had only drunk a total of 180ml (6oz) of milk since her last breast feed at 2pm the previous day. I knew that if she did not take a reasonable amount from a bottle soon, I would have to give up and allow her a breast feed. I gave her a dummy to keep her calm while I heated up the bottle feed, but she was so exhausted that she started to fall asleep. When the formula was the right temperature, I quickly replaced the dummy with the bottle and she took 210ml (7oz) without stopping. I was so concerned that she would throw it all up that I continued to hold her upright in my arms until 6.30am, when Eliza awoke.

Both the mother and I agreed that now Emily had taken a full feed from the bottle, it was better to keep on with the bottle and not to let her have the breast again. Neither of us felt we would have the strength to cope with a repeat of the previous night; the sanity of the family as a whole depended on both the parents and the babies getting some sleep. Continuing to breast feed was not an option the mother could even consider at this stage, so the breast milk she was producing had to be reduced gradually. With our experience of how each baby had responded to the bottle, we decided that it would be easier to allow Eliza to reduce the milk supply by going gradually from breast to bottle. If Emily was allowed on the breast again, it might prove even more difficult to persuade her to take the bottle.

By the end of the first week Emily was having three good bottle feeds a day, and had taken happily to the cup at the lunch-time feed. Eliza was now on a breast feed in the morning and one in the evening. She would also drink happily from a cup at lunch-time, and take a small bottle of formula at the 2.30pm feed. As with all my babies, I kept the 2.30pm feed small to ensure they both fed well at 6pm. Giving too large a feed at 2.30pm, or feeding later than 2.30pm in the day, are major contributory factors in most sleeping and feeding problems.

The mother's milk supply diminished very quickly, and I was convinced that she probably had not produced enough at the 6pm feed to satisfy two babies. They were now both on track with their milk feeding and solids and I felt confident that it was time to tackle the night waking. This was down to once a night, normally around 3am. As their day feeding had improved, they had graduated from sugar water to plain, cool boiled water. Emily normally woke first, and I was sure that it was her crying that caused Eliza to wake. On the tenth night I decided that I was going to let them settle themselves back to sleep when they awoke. Emily woke as usual on the dot of 3am screaming, and was joined very soon by Eliza. Both babies screamed on and off for over an hour, before settling back to sleep until 6.40am. The second night Emily woke again at 3am, but this time settled back to sleep within 25 minutes. Eliza stirred when she heard Emily crying but did not wake up and both babies had to be woken at 7am. On the third night both babies slept right through until 7am. I did hear them stirring between 3am and 4am, but neither of them cried.

They both continued to sleep well at nights, but the lunch-time nap was more difficult to crack. It took over a month to establish a really good nap, as both babies would wake up crying when they came into their light sleep 45 minutes after going to sleep. Eventually I persuaded the mother to hang a piece of black-out lining over the window, as I felt the light shining through the very thin blind did not help. There was an immediate improvement, and although they still woke up they settled back to sleep much sooner.

I am pleased to say that within a month there was also a slight improvement in their eczema. Five years later both girls are still sleeping well. They both still suffer from eczema, but the mother manages to control it with the use of creams and by watching their diet and ensuring their bedding is free from house mites.

Routine for a baby at nine to twelve months

Feed times	Nap times between 7am and 7pm
7am	9–9.45am
11.45am	12.30–2.30pm
2.30pm	
5pm	
6.30pm	**Maximum daily sleep 3 hours**

7am
- **Baby should be awake, nappy changed and feeding no later than 7am.**
- He should feed from both breasts or have a drink of formula from a cup, followed by breakfast cereal mixed with either expressed milk or formula and fruit.
- He should stay awake for two to two and a half hours.

8am
- He should be encouraged to have a kick on his play mat for 20–30 minutes.
- Wash and dress baby, remembering to cream all his creases and dry skin.

9am
- **Settle baby in the dark with the door shut no later than 9.30am.** He needs a sleep of 30–45 minutes.

9.30–9.45am
- Open the curtains so that he can wake up naturally.

10am
- **Baby must be fully awake now, regardless of how long he slept.**
- Encourage him to have a good kick under his play gym or take him on an outing.

11.45am

- He should be given most of his solids before being offered a drink of water or well-diluted juice from a cup, then alternate between solids and a drink.
- Encourage him to sit in his chair while you clear away the lunch things.

12.20pm

- Check the draw sheet and change his nappy.
- Close the curtains and **settle baby, in the dark with the door shut, no later than 12.30pm.**

12.30pm–2.30pm

- **He will need a nap now of no longer than two hours from the time he went down.**
- If he slept the full 45 minutes earlier he may need less sleep at this nap.

2.30pm

- **Baby must be awake and feeding no later than 2.30pm regardless of how long he has slept.**
- Open the curtains, and allow him to wake naturally. Change his nappy.
- He needs a breast feed or a drink of formula milk, water or well-diluted juice from a cup.
- **Do not feed him after 3.15pm as it will put him off his next feed.**

4.15pm

- Change baby's nappy, and offer him a drink of cool boiled water or well-diluted juice no later than 4.30pm.

5pm

- He should be given most of his solids before being offered a small drink of water or milk from a cup. It is important that he still has a good milk feed at bedtime, so keep this drink to a minimum.

6pm

- He must start his bath no later than 6pm, and be massaged and dressed no later than 6.30pm.

6.30pm

- **Baby must be feeding no later than 6.30pm.**
- He should feed from both breasts or have 210ml (7oz) of formula milk; this will eventually reduce to 150–180ml (5–6oz) when a cup is introduced at one year.
- Dim the lights and sit him in his chair for ten minutes while you tidy up.

7pm

- Settle him in his cot, in the dark with the door shut, no later than 7pm.

Changes to be made during the nine to twelve-month routine

Sleep

The majority of babies cut right back on their morning nap at this stage and may only need a catnap between 9.30 and 9.45am for 10–15 minutes. Some babies may also cut back their lunch-time nap to one and a half hours, which can lead to them being very tired and irritable late afternoon. If this happens to your baby, try cutting out the morning nap altogether to see if it improves his lunch-time sleep. You may have to bring lunch-time forward slightly if he can't make it through to 12.30pm for his nap.

Your baby may also start to pull himself up in the cot, but get very upset when he can't get himself back down. If this happens it would be advisable to encourage him to practise lying himself down when you put him down for his naps. Until he is able to manoeuvre himself up and down you will need to go in and help him settle back down. It is important that this is done with the least fuss and talking.

Feeding

If your baby starts to cut back on his last milk feed, reduce or cut out altogether the 2.30pm feed. Many babies cut out the 2.30pm feed by one year. As long as he is getting a minimum of 350ml (12oz) of milk a day inclusive of milk used in cereal and cooking, he will be getting enough.

He should be well established on three meals a day, and should also be able to feed himself some of the time. At nine months he should be taking his breakfast milk and 2.30pm feed from a cup.

By the age of one year he should be drinking all his milk and other fluids from a cup.

Lucy: aged nine months

Lucy was a third baby and was totally breast fed. She would not settle at 7pm and it would often take three hours of feeding and rocking before she went off to sleep. She would then wake several more times in the night, and need to be breast fed to get back to sleep. I agreed to move in for six days to try and help sort Lucy out, on the one condition that the mother was prepared to allow controlled crying. I also insisted that Lucy be given a bottle of formula at 7pm instead of the breast, as I was convinced that she was probably not getting enough to drink at that feed. Reluctantly her mother agreed to this.

On the first night she took 210ml (7oz) of formula, and settled well at 7.30pm. At 8.15pm she came into a light sleep and whimpered on and off for ten minutes. Her mother was very anxious and felt we should check her and I agreed to this as I wanted to see how her mother normally dealt with the situation. On entering the room she switched the lights on, and as Lucy had rolled on to her tummy her mother proceeded to roll her over on to her back again. I explained that a baby of Lucy's age must be allowed to sleep in the position that they find the most comfortable. She was very concerned about cot death, but agreed to allow Lucy to sleep on her tummy once she had read the literature from the Cot Death Foundation (see Useful Addresses).

I also reassured the mother that we knew Lucy had been well fed, so when she woke in the night I would settle her with water. She stirred several times in the night, whimpering but never crying. We had to wake her at 7am, and because her mother had not been feeding her on and off all night, she enjoyed a very big breast feed. I explained that at nine months Lucy did not need to be breast fed at lunchtime; once protein is introduced at lunchtime, the milk feed should be replaced with a drink of water or well-diluted juice from a cup. Lucy slept well after her lunch, and had the next breast feed at 2.30pm. I knew her mother was very keen to continue breast feeding, so I suggested that she give Lucy both breasts after her tea at 5pm. However, I felt it was important to top Lucy up with formula at bedtime.

As on the previous night, she drank 210ml (7oz) of formula and settled well. She stirred several times during the night, but only whimpered, never cried. During my six-night stay I never had to go to Lucy once, and each night she slept from 7.30pm to 7am.

While her mother was obviously not producing enough milk to settle Lucy at 7pm, I feel much of the night waking was brought on by her mother rushing to Lucy every time she came into a light sleep and chattered or whimpered. Lucy obviously preferred sleeping on her tummy and rolled over when she came into the light sleep. By forcing Lucy onto her back during this light sleep her mother was actually waking her fully, and the only way to calm her down was to put her to the breast.

Introducing solid food | 8

Weaning your baby

When to wean

Next to sleep, weaning is probably the most emotive subject in baby care. Between two and three months, just as you are beginning to see a regular pattern of milk feeding and sleep evolve, someone will bring up the subject of weaning. It is around this age that most babies discover their hands. This can lead to endless sucking, chewing and dribbling. Well-meaning grandparents and friends voice concern that your baby is hungry and not satisfied on milk alone. While this is one of the signs that a baby is ready to be weaned, it is by no means the only indicator. Do not be pressured into giving your baby solids unless you are absolutely sure he is ready.

It takes up to four months for the lining of the baby's gut to develop and for the kidneys to mature enough to cope with the waste products from solid food. If solids are introduced before a baby has the complete set of enzymes required to digest food properly, his digestive system could become damaged. Many experts blame the rapid increase in allergies over the last 20 years on babies being weaned before their digestive system is ready to cope. The most recent report from the Department of Health states that there is sufficient scientific evidence that exclusive breastfeeding for six months is nutritionally adequate for babies. It acknowledges, however, that introduction of solids at four months (17 weeks) is normal practice in the UK and recommends this as the earliest age at which weaning should begin. The guidelines acknowledge that the circumstances of mothers vary and that all babies are different. It is very important that weaning should not begin before neuro-muscular co-ordination has developed sufficiently, so that he can control his head and neck while sitting upright supported in a chair to be fed. He should also be able to swallow food easily, by moving it from the front of the mouth to the back.

In accordance with the advice given by experts and my own personal experience, I hope the following guidelines will help you decide if your baby is ready to be weaned. If he is four months old and weighs 12–14lb, he is probably ready to begin taking a small amount of solids if he is constantly showing most of the following signs:

- If he has been feeding well and going four hours between feeds during the day, but now gets very irritable and chews his hands an hour or so before his next feed is due.
- He is bottle fed and taking in more than 1140ml (38oz) per day but still appears to be hungry after a full feed of 240ml (8oz), four times a day.
- He usually sleeps well at night and nap times, but is waking up earlier and earlier.

If you choose to wait until six months before introducing solids you will need to introduce foods in larger amounts and give your baby new foods every couple of days. You might also find he goes back to needing a 10pm feed again, possibly even a 5am feed.

Breast-fed babies

With a baby who is being fully breast fed it is more difficult to tell how much milk he is receiving. If he is over four months and showing most of the above signs, I would probably wean him.

If he is under four months and not gaining enough weight each week, it is possible that your milk supply is getting very low later in the evening. All that may be needed is extra milk. I suggest you try topping up the baby with a couple of ounces of formula after the 10pm feed. If this does not work or if he is waking up more than once in the night, I would replace the

10pm feed altogether with a full bottle feed. Encourage your partner to do this feed so that you can get to bed early, after expressing whatever milk you have at 9pm to avoid your supply dropping any further. Mothers in this situation often find that when they express, they are only producing 90–120ml (3–4oz), which is much less than what their baby may need at this feed. The milk expressed can, if necessary, be given at some other feed during the day, thus avoiding further complementary bottle feeding.

This plan usually satisfies the baby's hunger, improves his weight gain and gets him through to four months before you need to introduce solids.

First stage:
four to six months

Studies into weaning by the University of Surrey revealed that babies fed diets with a high fruit content may be more prone to diarrhoea, which leads to slow growth. They advise that baby rice is the best first weaning food as fruit may not be so well tolerated by the underdeveloped gut of some babies.

I always start weaning at the 11am feed with a teaspoon of pure organic baby rice mixed with either a small amount of the formula or some expressed breast milk. I find it best to give the baby most of his milk feed first, then offer the baby rice followed by the rest of the milk.

By day 14 of weaning he should be having up to 1 cube of carrot purée at lunch, and up to 3 level teaspoons of baby rice plus 1 cube of pear purée at 6pm. He should continue to have most of his milk first, at least 210ml (7oz) before the solids.

Introduce a further fruit at lunch time, either apple or peach. After three days transfer to the evening meal and introduce sweet potato with the carrot at lunch-time for a further three days.

Weaning: Days 1–15

Days	Time	Food
1–3	11am	Breast feed or 180–240ml (6–8oz) of formula milk 1 tsp of pure organic baby rice mixed with breast milk, formula or cool boiled water
4–6	6pm	Breast feed or 180–240ml (6–8oz) of formula milk 1–2 tsp baby rice mixed with breast milk, formula or cool boiled water
7–9	11am	Breast feed or 180–240ml (6–8oz) of formula milk 1 cube of carrot purée
	6pm	Breast feed or 180–210ml (6–7oz) of formula milk 1–2 tsp baby rice mixed with breast milk, formula or cool boiled water plus 1 cube of pear purée
10–12	11am	Breast feed or 180–240ml (6–8oz) of formula milk 1 cube of apple purée
	6pm	Breast feed or 210–240ml (7–8oz) of formula milk 2–3 tsp baby rice mixed with breast milk, formula or cool boiled water
13–15	11am	Breast feed or 180–240ml (6–8oz) of formula milk 1 cube of sweet potato purée
	6pm	Breast feed or 210–240ml (7–8oz) of formula milk 2–3 tsp baby rice mixed with breast milk, formula or cool boiled water plus 1 cube of pear purée

Start to alternate the fruit at night time. From now on introduce a new vegetable every three days at lunch time, alternating with the ones he is already eating.

Note: To avoid problems with baby's digestion, new foods must only be introduced every three days. It is vital to remember that milk is still the most important food at this stage. By replacing it too quickly with solid food you will deny your baby the perfect balance of vitamins and minerals that milk supplies. By using the above method during the first month of weaning you can be sure your baby will take exactly the amount of solids that he needs, without losing the nutritional value of the milk.

Once the baby is established on rice at 11am and shows no reaction I would transfer the rice to after the 6pm feed. I then introduce a teaspoonful of puréed organic pear after the 11am feed. If it is tolerated, after three days I would mix the pear with the rice at the 6pm feed. This makes the rice more palatable and avoids the baby becoming constipated. I now begin to introduce a small amount of various organic vegetables and fruit after the 11am feed. I am convinced that the reason very few of my babies develop a sweet tooth is because they are given more vegetables than fruit in the early days of weaning. The vegetables favoured by most babies at this stage are carrots, sweet potato, green beans, courgettes and swede or turnip.

Other foods

Gillian Harris, a clinical psychologist researching weaning in babies, found that babies introduced to a wide variety of non-allergy-forming foods from the age of four months would accept a wider range of foods at one year than those weaned on a restricted diet. I agree with this, as I have found that babies who are allowed excessive quantities of milk between four and six months and are not encouraged to enjoy solids usually end up very fussy eaters.

Between the ages of five and six months babies who started weaning at four months should have tasted cereal, plus a variety of vegetables and fruit from the ones listed in the first stage on page 192. Food still needs to be puréed, but not so smoothly. This will help prepare your baby for mashed food at six months.

Meat, chicken or fish should not be introduced until the baby is capable of digesting reasonable amounts of other solids. Some nutritionists believe that protein can put a strain on the young baby's kidneys and digestive tract. I agree with this, as all too often I have seen feeding problems occur because meat, poultry or fish have been introduced too early. A very large baby could start protein at around five months, but for most, six months is the best age.

Dairy products, wheat, eggs, nuts and citrus fruits should still be avoided at this stage, as they are the foods most likely to trigger allergies. Salt should be avoided and sugar only used in small quanties when stewing very sour fruit. Honey should not be introduced before one year.

Breakfast

A baby is ready to start having breakfast once he shows signs of hunger long before his 11am feed. This usually happens between the ages of five and six months. All cereal should be wheat and gluten free until the age of six months. I find that organic oatmeal cereal with a small amount of puréed fruit is a favourite with most babies.

You should still give your baby most of his milk feed first; after a couple of weeks give about two-thirds of his milk feed first, then the cereal, finishing up with the remainder of the milk feed. If your baby reaches six months and shows no sign of wanting breakfast, it would be wise to reduce his milk feed very slightly and offer a small amount of solids.

Daily requirements

By six months, most babies are enjoying at least two meals a day and heading towards a third. If your baby is not showing much interest in solids but is drinking a lot of milk, it would be wise to cut back on his lunch-time feed to encourage his interest in the solids. Some babies get really hooked on milk and hate the feel of a spoon in their mouth and start to refuse solid food altogether.

Your baby still needs a minimum of 600ml (20oz) of breast or formula milk a day.

Molly: aged six months

Molly was difficult to settle in the evening and would wake up two to three times in the night. She drank very little milk and screamed when fed solids. Because she was very underweight for her age, she had been admitted to hospital at the age of five months to see if tests could find the cause of the sleeping and feeding problems. The spell in hospital confirmed that there was nothing physically wrong with Molly, but because of her low weight gain the parents were advised to continue to feed little and often, and on demand. She would, they said, 'eventually sort herself out'. Easy advice to give if you are not the one being deprived of sleep night after night, and trying to cope with a fractious baby and a toddler during the day.

As is my usual practice, I observed the mum and baby the first day. Because of her disruptive nights, Molly normally started her day at 8.30am. She would drink around 90ml (3oz) of formula, followed by a small amount of packet breakfast cereal. Molly would then be awake for at least four hours, most of which time was spent whinging or crying, and she had to be carried or held the whole time. At 11am she would be given another bottle feed, then a jar of either chicken casserole or beef stew. As with breakfast, she would only take 60ml (2oz) of milk and a few spoonfuls of solids before she started screaming and straining. She had suffered from constipation since being weaned at three months.

Her mother would usually end up by putting her in her pram in the kitchen and rocking her to sleep. Molly had never slept more than one hour at this time of the day, and would normally wake up screaming. Her mother, concerned about her low milk intake, would offer her a bottle of formula immediately she woke. This would be her best feed of the day and she would drink around 180ml (6oz), then fall asleep, exhausted, for at least two hours.

Her elder sister arrived home from school around now, and usually managed to keep Molly entertained while their mother made the tea for both girls. At 4.30pm Molly would have a bowl of packet food, followed by approximately 120ml (4oz) of formula.

Both girls were taken upstairs around 5.30pm for their bath. After the bath, at about 6.30pm Molly was given a further bottle feed, of which she would usually drink 90–120ml (3–4oz), and fall straight to sleep. She would then wake up two hours later, take a further 60ml (2oz) and fall asleep until around one in the morning.

The parents had tried many times to waken her between 10pm and 11pm to give her a bottle in the hope that she would sleep through. She was always in such a deep sleep at this time that it was impossible to wake her enough to get her to drink more than 60ml (2oz) of formula. There were normally at least two other wakings in the night, and each time she would usually drink no more than 60ml (2oz). Eventually, at 5am Molly would settle into a deep sleep. The parents, exhausted after a night of broken sleep, were so desperate for sleep themselves that they would let her sleep until 8.30am, and on some occasions even 9am.

Molly was drinking on average a daily total of 720–780ml (24–26oz) of formula, which in itself would be fairly normal for a baby of her age. The problem was that nearly half of this amount was being drunk between 9pm and 5am, when she should have been drinking the whole amount between 7am and 7pm.

The other big concern was that her solid intake was very low, and nutritionally virtually nil. Molly was fed exclusively on packet food or jars, most of which have a high content of water, sugar and maltodextrin (something that is put on the back of postage stamps) and other fillers. Surveys done by the Food Commission confirm that the chicken content of some jars of chicken casserole is as low as 4 per cent. It is not surprising that Molly was way below her proper level on her growth chart.

I decided to take Molly right back to stage one of the weaning programme. My main aim was to get her to take a full formula milk feed first thing in the morning and in the evening, and to get her used to eating proper food. In order for her to be hungry enough in the morning I knew I had to get rid of the middle-of-the-night feeding. The first day I cut the 2.30pm feed, which was normally her best, right back to 90ml (3oz) and cut out her 4.30pm solids altogether. In the evening after her bath she took 180ml (6oz), which was more milk than normal. I also gave her two small spoonfuls of baby rice mixed with 30ml (1oz) of formula. She did not wake up at 9pm, but did wake as usual at 1pm and 4pm. Both times I offered her a small amount of sugared water and cuddled her back to sleep. She awoke at 6.45am and for the first time ever, very quickly drank a full 240ml (8oz) bottle of formula in ten minutes.

I decided not to give her breakfast for a few days until her bottle feeding and lunch and tea were properly established. At 11am, I offered her another 240ml (8oz) bottle of formula, of which she took 210ml (7oz), followed by a few spoonfuls of mashed potato and puréed carrot. When she awoke at 2.30pm I gave her a small feed of 150ml (5oz). I knew she would have taken more at this feed, but I deliberately wanted to keep it small to encourage her to take a really good feed at bedtime.

Around 5pm she became very irritable so I let her suck on a rusk, most of which went on the floor, but it did occupy her until bath time. After the bath at 6pm she gulped down 210ml (7oz) of formula, followed by baby rice and fruit purée.

For her sleep pattern that day I followed the routine for a four-month-old baby; this was to allow her time to settle herself to sleep. Apart from a few brief protests, she adapted to this very well. She yelled for 20 minutes when she went down at 7pm, and I did not hear another peep until 3am. Like the previous night, I offered her sugar water and cuddled her back to sleep. For the following three days I followed much the same routine. She gradually increased her solids until she was eating an acceptable amount for a baby of her age, and she continued to drink her bottle feed well.

By this time she was still waking once in the night, but only taking a small amount of plain, cool boiled water and settling back very quickly. I decided now was the time for her to learn how to settle herself in the night when she woke up. Her day-time naps were on routine and she was feeding well, so I felt confident she would get out of the habit of needing the water very quickly. The first night she cried on and off for 40 minutes, the next night for 30 minutes, and the last night 15 minutes. She then slept through from 7pm to 6.45am.

Two weeks later we dropped the 11am milk feed and reintroduced chicken casserole for lunch, but we found that she became very constipated again and started to fuss over her food. I suggested that we avoid giving her protein and starch at the same meal and this seemed to solve that problem.

We also had to continue giving her the solids after the 6pm bottle feed for a further three months. On the couple of occasions we gave her the solids at 5pm, she refused to drink a full feed at 6pm. This resulted in a 5am waking, instead of the usual 7am.

While Molly did have some wrong sleep association problems, I believe that they were not the main cause of the disruptive nights. I am convinced the real problems were poor structuring of milk feeds, and weaning too early on to the wrong type of solid food. I am pleased to say Molly started to gain weight and continued to sleep well.

Second stage: six to nine months

During the first stage of weaning, milk is still providing your baby with all the nutrients he needs. In the second stage of weaning, solids should gradually take over and provide more of your baby's daily nutritional needs. You should be aiming towards three well-balanced meals a day.

Most babies are ready to accept stronger tasting foods at this age. They also take pleasure from different textures, colours and presentation. Foods should be mashed or 'pulsed' and kept separate so that they avoid mixing everything up. Fruit need not be cooked; it can be grated or mashed. It is also around this age that your baby will begin to put food in his mouth. Raw soft fruit, lightly cooked vegetables and toast can be used as finger foods. They will be sucked and squeezed more than eaten at this stage, but allowing him the opportunity to feed himself encourages good feeding habits later on. Once your baby is having finger foods, always wash his hands before a meal and never leave him alone while he is eating.

Foods to introduce with caution

Chicken, fish and meat can be introduced at this stage. Check that all the bones are removed and trim off the fat and the skin. Some babies find the flavour of protein cooked on its own too strong. Try cooking chicken or meat in a casserole, and fish in a milk sauce until your baby becomes accustomed to the different texture and taste.

Dairy products and wheat can also be introduced at this stage. Full-fat cow's milk can be used in cooking, but should not be given as a drink until one year. All these foods should be introduced gradually and careful notes made of any reactions.

Introducing a cup

Once protein is introduced at lunchtime, the milk feed must be replaced by a drink of water or well-diluted juice from a cup. Most babies of six months are capable of sipping and swallowing, and this should be encouraged by being consistent and always offering the lunch-time drink from a cup. Do not worry if your baby only drinks a small amount at this meal; you will probably find that he makes up for it at his 2.30pm milk feed.

Breakfast

Sugar-free, unrefined wheat cereals can now be introduced; choose ones fortified with iron and B vitamins. Try adding a little mashed or grated fruit if your baby refuses them. You can encourage your baby with finger foods by offering him a little buttered toast at this stage. Most babies are still desperate for their milk first thing in the morning, so still allow him two-thirds of his milk first.

Lunch

At this stage, most babies are eating a proper breakfast and lunch comes a little later, somewhere between 11.45am and 12 noon. Once you introduce chicken or fish at lunchtime you should replace the milk feed with a drink of water or well-diluted juice from a cup. Encourage your baby to take most of his solids before offering him a drink. He needs one portion of protein a day, and lentils and pulses are good alternatives to chicken or fish.

Tea

During the second stage of weaning, the rice and fruit that has been given after the 6pm milk feed will be replaced with a proper tea at 5pm. This can consist of foods like mini sandwiches, or a baked potato or pasta served with vegetables and a sauce. Some babies get very tired and fussy by teatime. If you always make sure your baby has a well-balanced breakfast and lunch, you can be more relaxed about this meal. If your baby does not eat much, try offering some rice pudding or a yoghurt. A small drink of water from a cup can be offered after the tea. Do not allow too large a drink at this time as it will put him off his last milk feed.

His bedtime milk feed is still important at this stage. If he starts cutting back too much on this feed, check you are not overfeeding him on solids.

Daily requirements

At this stage your baby should be well on the way to eating three proper meals a day. They should include two to three servings of carbohydrates, such as cereals, bread and pasta, plus at least two servings of vegetables and fruit, and one serving of puréed meat, fish or pulses. By six months a baby has used up all the store of iron he was born with. As his requirements between six and 12 months are particularly high, it is important that his diet provides the right amount of iron. To help improve iron absorption in cereals and meat, always serve with fruit or vegetables and avoid giving milk to drink with protein as it reduces the iron content by 50 per cent.

He still needs 530–600ml (18–20oz) of breast or formula milk a day inclusive of milk used for mixing food. If your baby starts to reject his milk, try giving him more cheese, milk sauces and yoghurt.

Third stage:
nine to twelve months

Between nine and twelve months your baby should be eating and enjoying all types of food, with the exception of food with a high fat, salt or sugar content. Peanuts and honey should also still be avoided. It is very important that your baby learns to chew properly at this stage. Food should be chopped or diced, although meat still needs to be pulsed or very finely chopped. This is also a good time to introduce raw vegetables and salads.

Try to include some finger foods at every meal and if he shows an interest in holding his own spoon, do not discourage these attempts. It is important that he enjoys his meals, even if a certain amount of them lands on the floor. Always supervise your baby while he is feeding himself.

Breakfast

Encourage your baby to take at least some of his breakfast milk feed from a cup. By the end of the first year he should be drinking all of his breakfast milk from a cup. Aim to get him to take 210ml (7oz) of milk at this meal, divided between a drink and his breakfast cereal. Scrambled egg can be offered once or twice a week as a change.

Lunch

Lunch should consist of a wide selection of lightly steamed, chopped vegetables served with a daily serving of meat or meat alternative. Babies of this age are very active and can become quite tired and irritable by 5pm. By ensuring a well-balanced lunch, you will not need to worry if tea is more relaxed. By the end of the first year your baby's lunch can be integrated with the family lunch. Prepare the meal without salt, sugar or spices and reserve a portion for the baby, then add the desired flavourings for the rest of the family.

Try to ensure that his meals are attractively presented, with a variety of different coloured vegetables and fruit. Do not overload his plate; serve up a small amount and when he finishes that replenish his plate. This also helps to avoid the game of throwing food on the floor, which often occurs at this stage. If your baby does start to play up with his main course, refusing to eat and throwing his food on the floor, quietly and firmly say 'no', and remove the plate. Do not offer him a biscuit or fromage frais half an hour later, as a pattern will soon emerge where he will refuse his lunch knowing he will get something sweet if he plays up enough. A piece of fruit can be offered mid-afternoon to see him through to his tea, at which time he will probably eat very well.

A drink of well-diluted, pure unsweetened orange juice in a cup will help the absorption of iron at this meal, but make

sure that he has most of his meal before you allow him to finish the drink.

Tea

Many babies cut out their 2.30pm milk during this stage. If
you are worried that your baby's daily milk intake is too low,
try giving things like pasta and vegetables with a milk sauce,
baked potatoes with grated cheese, cheesy vegetable bake or
mini quiches at teatime. Teatime is usually the meal when I
would give small helpings of milk pudding or fromage frais,
which are also alternatives if milk is being rejected. Try regularly to include some finger foods at teatime.

The bedtime bottle should be discouraged after one year,
so during this stage get your baby gradually used to less milk
at bedtime. This can be done by offering him a small drink of
milk with his teatime meal, then a drink of 150–180ml
(5–6oz) of milk from a cup at bedtime.

Daily requirements

By one year it is important that large volumes of milk are discouraged; no more than 600ml (20oz) inclusive of milk used
in food should be allowed. After one year your baby needs a
minimum of 350ml (12oz) a day. This is usually divided
between two or three drinks and inclusive of milk used in
cooking or on cereals.

Full-fat, pasteurized cow's milk can be given to drink after
one year. If your baby refuses cow's milk, try gradually dilut-
ing his formula with it until he is happy to take full cow's
milk. If possible try to give your baby organic cow's milk as
it comes from cows fed exclusively on grass, unlike unorgan-
ic milk where the cows are fed on a diet of animal offal. The
cows have difficulty in digesting the meat, the undigested
meat is turned into mucus in the digestive system and is
excreted via the udders, resulting in milk with a mucus content as high as 30 per cent compared to the mucus content of
5 per cent found in organic milk.

Encourage three well-balanced meals a day and avoid
snacks of biscuits, cakes and crisps.

Your questions answered

Q At what age would you wean a baby onto solids?

A • The majority of babies do not need solid food before four months.

• Occasionally a larger baby weighing more than 14lb at three months may need to be weaned.

• If I do have to wean a baby before four months, I keep the food very simple, i.e. pure organic baby rice and puréed organic pear, until he reaches four months.

Q How will I know when my baby is ready to be weaned?

A • If your baby has been sleeping through and starts to wake up in the night or very early in the morning, and will not settle back to sleep.

• A bottle-fed baby taking in excess of 960–1140ml (32–38oz) a day, draining a 240ml (8oz) bottle each feed and looking for another feed long before it is due.

• A breast-fed baby would start to look for a feed every two to three hours.

• Both breast- and bottle-fed babies would start to chew on their hands a lot and be very irritable in between feeds.

• If unsure, always talk to your health visitor or paediatrician.

Q What would happen if I weaned my baby before he was ready?

A • His digestive system could be harmed if he has not developed the complete set of enzymes required to digest solids.

• Introducing solids before he is ready could lead to allergies.

• Studies from several different countries show that persistent coughs and wheezing are more common in babies who were weaned before 12 weeks.

Q At which milk feed should I introduce solids?

A • I usually start at the 11am feed as this feed will gradually be pushed to 12 noon, becoming a proper lunch once solids become established.

• Milk is still the most important source of food. By giving solids after this feed you can be sure that your baby will have at least half of his daily milk intake before noon.

• Solids offered at the 2.30pm feed seem to put babies off the very important 6pm feed.

• If a very hungry baby has no reaction to the baby rice within three days, I would then transfer the rice to after the 6pm feed.

Q Which is the best food to introduce?

A • I find pure organic baby rice is the food that satisfies most babies' hunger the best. If this is tolerated I would then introduce some organic puréed pear.

• Once these two foods are established, it is best to concentrate on introducing a variety of vegetables from the First Stage on pages 191–3.

• In a survey carried out by the University of Surrey it was found that babies weaned on fruit were less likely to thrive than those weaned on baby rice. They advise that all babies should start weaning on baby rice.

Q How will I know how much solid food to give my baby?

A • For the first six months, milk is still the most important part of your baby's diet. It will provide him with the right balance of vitamins and minerals, so he will need a minimum of 600ml (20oz) a day. During the first month of weaning, if you always offer the milk feed first, then the solids, you can be sure he will take exactly the amount of solids he needs. This avoids him replacing his milk too quickly with solids.

- Between five and six months you can start at the 11am feed to give half the milk feed first, then some solids followed by more milk. This will encourage your baby to cut back slightly on his milk feed and increase his solids, preparing him for a feeding pattern of three meals a day at six months.
- With breast-fed babies a feed from one breast can be classed as half a milk feed.

Q At what age should I start to reduce the amount of milk he drinks?
A • Up to the age of six months your baby still needs a minimum of 600ml (20oz) of milk a day. From five months more milk will be used to mix his rice, cereal and solids, so the actual amount he drinks reduces slightly, but his daily intake should remain much the same.
- As he increases his solids, the feeds he should cut back on are the 11am and 2.30pm.
- Your baby should be established on the tier system at lunch-time by six months.
- Once your baby is established on three meals a day, introduce the tier-system breakfast (see page 173).

Q At what age do I start to cut out milk feeds altogether?
A • Assuming your baby was on five milk feeds when he started to wean, once he increases his solids after the 6pm feed, he should automatically cut back on his 10pm feed, and cut it out altogether somewhere between four and five months.
- The next feed to cut out would be the 11–11.30am feed. Once your baby is having chicken or fish for lunch the milk feed should be replaced with a drink of water or well-diluted juice from a cup.
- The 2.30pm feed often increases for a few months, then somewhere between nine and twelve months he will lose interest in this feed, at which time it can be dropped.

Q **At what age would you introduce a drinking cup and at which feeds?**

A • Between the age of six and seven months is the best time.

• When you have replaced the lunch-time milk feed with water or well-diluted juice, try giving it from a cup or a bottle with a hard spout.

• Try half way through the meal and after every few spoonfuls of food.

• It is important to persevere. Experiment with different types of cup until you find one with which your baby is happy.

• Once he is taking a few ounces from a cup, gradually introduce it at other feeds.

• It is generally recommended that bottle feeding be discouraged after one year, as it will stop the appetite for other foods.

Q **When can I introduce cow's milk?**

A • I usually introduce a small amount of organic cow's milk in cooking from six months. It can be used in cooking from four months.

• Cow's milk should not be given as a drink until your baby is at least one year old.

• It should always be full-fat pasteurized milk.

• If your baby refuses cow's milk, try mixing half the amount with formula. Once he is happy taking that, gradually increase the cow's milk until he is happy with all cow's milk.

Q **At what age can I stop puréeing his food?**

A • Around the age of six to seven months I start to mash the vegetables and fruit really well, so that there are no lumps, but it is not as smooth as the puréed food.

• Between six and nine months I gradually mash the food

less and less until the baby will take food with lumps in it.

- Chicken and meat should still be pulsed until your baby is around ten months old.

Q When will he be able to manage finger foods?
A • From six months of age most babies are capable of eating a small amount of finger foods.
- He should be offered small pieces of softly cooked vegetables or pieces of soft fruit.
- Once he is managing vegetables and fruit, offer a piece of toast or a rusk.
- By nine months encourage a variety of lightly cooked or raw foods in the form of finger foods or chopped with his main meal.

Q At what age will he be able to feed himself with a spoon?
A • Once your baby starts to grab at the spoon, give him one to hold.
- When he repeatedly puts it in his mouth, load up another spoon and let him try to get it into his mouth, quickly popping in any food that falls out with your spoon.
- With a little help and guidance most babies from 12 months are capable of feeding themselves with part of their meal.
- Always supervise your baby during meal times. Never, ever leave him alone.

Q When can I stop sterilizing?
A • Bottles should be sterilized until your baby is one year old.
- Dishes and spoons can stop being sterilized when your baby is six months. They can then be put in the dishwasher, or washed thoroughly in hot soapy water, then rinsed and left to air dry.
- Between four and six months, the pots, cooking utensils

and ice cube trays used for preparing weaning food can either be put in the dishwasher or washed in hot soapy water, rinsed and then have boiled water poured over them before being left to air dry.

Q Which foods are most likely to cause allergies and what are the main symptoms?

A • The most common foods that cause allergies are dairy products, wheat, fish, eggs and citrus fruits.

• Symptoms include rashes, wheezing, coughing, running nose, sore bottom, diarrhoea, irritability and swelling of the eyes.

• Keeping a detailed record when you are weaning can be a big help when you are trying to establish the cause of any of the above symptoms.

• The above symptoms can also be caused by the house mite, animal fur, wool and certain soaps and household cleaning agents.

• If in doubt, always check with your doctor to rule out any other possible causes or illness for the above symptoms.

Feeding plan at four to five months

	Week 1	Week 2	Week 3	Week 4
Introduce	Rice	Apple	Sweet potato	Courgettes
	Pear	Carrot	Green beans	Swede

• When preparing food always ensure that all surfaces are clean and have been wiped down with an anti-bacterial cleaner. Use kitchen roll for cleaning surfaces and drying, as it is more hygienic than kitchen cloths and towels, which may carry bacteria.

- All fresh fruit and vegetables should be carefully peeled, removing the core, pips and any blemishes. They should then be rinsed thoroughly with filtered water.
- All fruit and vegetables must be cooked until your baby is six months old. This can be done by either steaming or boiling in filtered water. Do not add salt, sugar or honey.
- At this stage all food must be cooked until soft enough to purée to a very smooth consistency. A small amount of the cooking water may need to be added so that the mixture is similar to smooth yoghurt.
- If using a food processor check carefully for lumps by using a spoon and pouring into another bowl. Then transfer to ice cube trays or containers for storage in the freezer.
- Freshly prepared food should be cooled quickly and put in the freezer or fridge as soon as possible after cooking.
- Whether using fresh produce, packets or jars, try whenever possible to buy organic produce, which is free from preservatives and pesticides. Avoid packets with artificial flavourings, added sugars or fillers like maltodextrin.
- Introduce solids after the 11am feed. Prepare in advance everything needed for giving the solids: baby chair, two bibs, two spoons and a clean, fresh damp cloth.
- Always offer the milk first, as milk is still the most important food at this stage. It provides your baby's nutritional needs with the right balance of vitamins and minerals.
- Solids at this stage are only first tastes and fillers, which prepare your baby for three meals a day. His daily milk intake should not decrease at this stage.
- Food should be heated thoroughly to ensure that any bacteria are killed. If using jars, always transfer the required amount to a dish; never serve straight from the jar. Any food left over in the dish or jar should be discarded, never reheated and used again.
- Make sure food is cooled enough before feeding it to your baby.
- Use a shallow plastic spoon, never a metal one, which can be too sharp or get too hot.

- Some babies need help in learning how to feed from the spoon. By placing the spoon just far enough into his mouth and bringing the spoon up and out against the roof of his mouth, his upper gums will take off the food, encouraging him to feed.
- Always be very positive and smile when offering new foods. If your baby spits it out, it may not mean he dislikes it. This is all very new him and different foods get different reactions. If he positively refuses a food, leave it and try again in a week.
- Introduce a new food every three to four days so that you can see how your baby reacts to each new food.
- Encourage more vegetables than fruit, but avoid strong tasting ones like broccoli and spinach at this stage. Concentrate on the root vegetables listed in the feeding plan (see page 208), which are naturally sweeter.
- By the end of the first month lunch should be made up of a selection of vegetables and sweet potato. Supper would be organic baby rice and fruit purée.
- Be guided by your baby as to when to increase the amounts. He will turn his head away and get fussy when he has had enough.
- He still needs a minimum of 600ml (20oz) a day of breast milk or formula, so keep giving him the milk first to ensure that you do not increase solids too quickly.
- Encourage him to sit in his chair and entertain himself while you clear up. Any cloths used to wash his face and hands should be put straight to soak with the bibs to avoid bacteria build-up.
- By five months his day's menu may look something like the following:

Breakfast	Breast feed or 180–240ml (6–8oz) of formula milk
Lunch	Breast feed or 180–240ml (6–8oz) of formula milk
	Sweet potato with one other vegetable
Afternoon	Breast feed or 150–210ml (5–7oz) of formula milk
Evening	Breast feed or 210–240ml (7–8oz) formula milk
	Baby rice with a small amount of fruit purée

Feeding plan at
five to six months

	Week 1	Week 2	Week 3	Week 4
Introduce	Oats	Parsnip	Mango	Peas
	Peaches	Avocado	Barley	Cauliflower

- All fruit and vegetables should still be steamed or cooked in filtered water until soft, then puréed. Mix to the desired consistency with some of the cooking water, or chicken stock may be used with vegetables.
- Introduce some oat cereal mixed with some of your baby's first milk feed and fruit purée for breakfast.
- Once breakfast is introduced he should be happy to go longer between his feeds. Gradually keep pushing the 11am feed later until he is eating lunch between 11.45am and 12 noon.
- Once he is eating lunch at a later time, you can start to use the tier method of feeding (see page 112), alternating between his milk and the solids.
- Once the tier method of eating is introduced at lunch time the solids should start to overtake the milk. Keep increasing the solids and gradually reduce the milk feed, preparing him to drop it once protein is introduced at six months.
- In the evening make sure he still has at least 210–240ml (7–8oz) of formula or both breasts for his last feed at 6–7pm.
- Milk intake may have dropped slightly, but he still needs a minimum of 600ml (20oz) a day of breast or formula milk.
- By six months his day's menu may look something like the following:

Breakfast	Breast feed or 210–240ml (7–8oz) of formula milk
	Oat cereal with fruit purée
Lunch	Breast feed or 150–210ml (5–7oz) of formula milk
	Potato or barley cereal mixed with a selection of other vegetables

Afternoon	Breast feed or 150–180ml (5–6oz) of formula milk
Evening	Breast feed or 210–240ml (7–8oz) of formula milk
	Baby rice or gluten-free cereal with a small amount of fruit purée

Feeding plan at six to seven months

	Week 1	Week 2	Week 3	Week 4
Introduce	Chicken	Lentils	Cheddar cheese	Fish
	Broccoli	Asparagus	Peas	Bananas
	Yoghurt	Wheat	Brown rice	Peppers

- Each day your baby should have two to three servings of carbohydrates in the form of cereal, wholemeal bread, pasta or potatoes.
- Cereal should be less refined now. Choose sugar-free ones rich in iron and vitamins such as Weetabix or Ready Brek, served with mashed fresh fruit.
- Cheese should be full fat, pasteurized and grated, and preferably organic.
- Your baby should have at least three servings of vegetables and fruit a day and he will also need one serving of animal or vegetable protein.
- Meat and poultry should have all fat, skin and bones removed. Cook with vegetables as a casserole and pulse in a food processor.
- Vegetables should be mashed now, not puréed and most fruit can be served raw, either mashed or grated.
- Introduce small amounts of finger foods: cubes of raw soft fruit or cooked vegetables. Once he manages these, toast or rusks can also be offered but make sure you wash his hands thoroughly before and after the meal.

- When he is having protein at lunch time, the milk feed should be replaced with a drink of water or well-diluted juice – try to encourage him to drink from a cup.
- A very hungry baby may need a small drink and a piece of fruit mid-morning. Small amounts of butter and full-fat cow's milk (preferably organic) can be used in cooking, but cow's milk should not be given as a drink yet as it is too low in iron.
- He still needs 530–600ml (18–20oz) of breast or formula milk each day, inclusive of milk used in sauces and cereals.
- By the end of six months your baby will probably be ready to sit in a high chair for his meals.
- If your baby has cut any teeth, they should be cleaned twice a day.
- By 7 months his day's menu may look something like the following:

Breakfast	Breast feed or 210–240ml (7–8oz) of formula milk
	Wholewheat or oat cereal with milk and fruit *or*
	Baby muesli with milk and fruit
	Toast with fruit spread
Lunch	Chicken casserole *or*
	Steamed fish with creamed vegetables *or*
	Vegetable and lentil shepherd's pie *or*
	Chicken risotto *or*
	Chicken with asparagus and peach purée
	Drink of water or well-diluted juice from a cup
Mid-afternoon	Breast feed or 150–210ml (5–7oz) of formula milk
Tea	Baked potato with creamed vegetables *or*
	Pasta and vegetables with a sauce *or*
	Thick barley broth *or*
	Pasta with red pepper sauce
	Bread, rusks or rice cakes with a savoury spread
	Milk pudding or yoghurt
	Small drink of water from a cup
Bedtime	Breast feed or 180–240ml (6–8oz) of formula milk

Feeding plan at
seven to eight months

	Week 1	Week 2	Week 3	Week 4
Introduce	Soya	Lamb	Beans	Cabbage
	Apricots	Melon	Plums	Tomatoes
	Pumpkin	Spinach	Vegetable oil	Herbs

- Each day your baby should have two to three servings of carbohydrates in the form of cereal, wholemeal bread, pasta or potatoes.
- He should also have at least three servings of vegetables and fruit each day and will need one serving of animal protein or two of vegetable protein.
- He should be eating three well-balanced meals a day and drinking three milk feeds from the breast, bottle or cup. The 2.30pm feed should be established from the cup by eight months.
- All fruit and vegetables should be mashed or pulsed and dried fruit should be washed thoroughly and soaked first.
- Olive oil can be used when cooking casseroles and by the end of eight months small quantities of herbs can be used in cooking.
- Continue to offer finger foods such as pieces of raw soft fruits, lightly cooked vegetables and bread, rusks or toast with savoury spread.
- Try to get him to drink all his well-diluted juice or water from a cup. A bottle fed baby should be encouraged to drink some of his breakfast milk from a cup, but he still needs to feed from both breasts or have a 180–210ml (6–7oz) bottle feed at 6.30pm.
- If he refuses or cuts right back on his last milk feed try cutting down on his 2.30pm milk feed. If this fails, replace the 2.30pm feed with well-diluted juice, as if he cuts out a milk feed it is better to do so at 2.30pm than at 6.30pm.

- He still needs a minimum of 530–600ml (18–20oz) of breast milk or formula each day. If he is not taking this amount, introduce more cheese sauces, milk puddings or yoghurt.
- By eight months his day's menu may look something like the following:

Breakfast	Breast feed or 180–240ml (6–8oz) of formula milk
	Wholewheat or oat cereal with milk and fruit *or*
	Baby muesli with milk and fruit *or*
	Toast with fruit spread *plus*
	Mixed fruit and yoghurt
Lunch	Lamb casserole with carrot and potato purée *or*
	Cod with broccoli and cheese sauce *or*
	Lentil and spinach lasagne *or*
	Chicken and tomato risotto *or*
	Lamb and barley hotpot
	Drink of water or well-diluted juice from a cup
Mid afternoon	Breast feed or 150–210ml (5–7oz) of formula milk
Tea	Minestrone and pasta soup *or*
	Cream of leek and potato soup *plus*
	Bread, rusks or rice cakes with a savoury spread *or*
	Butter bean casserole *or*
	Spinach and pasta bake
	Milk pudding or yoghurt
	Small drink of water from a cup
Bedtime	Breast feed or 210–240ml (7–8oz) of formula milk

Feeding plan at eight to nine months

	Week 1	Week 2	Week 3	Week 4
Introduce	Butter	Cottage cheese	Brussels sprouts	Prunes
	Liver	Guava	Figs	Oranges
	Margarine	Celery	Tuna fish	Egg yolk

- Each day your baby should have three servings of carbo-hydrates, made up of cereal, wholemeal bread, pasta or potatoes.
- He should have at least three portions of vegetables and fruit, including some raw chopped vegetables and will need one portion of animal protein or two of vegetable protein.
- Vegetables and fruit with a high vitamin C content should be served with protein meals; this aids iron absorp-tion.
- Figs and prunes should be washed thoroughly and soaked or stewed.
- Egg yolk can be introduced, but the egg should be hard boiled.
- Tuna fish in brine should be avoided as it has a high salt content. Choose tuna in vegetable oil.
- Your baby may show signs of wanting to feed himself. If so, use two spoons. Load one spoon for him to try and get the food into his mouth by himself and use the other spoon yourself to actually get the food in. Help his co-ordination by holding his wrist and gently guiding him.
- By the end of nine months a bottle-fed baby should be drinking all of his breakfast milk from a cup, but if he is losing interest in his milk, give him extra cheese, sauces or milk puddings.
- He still needs 530–600ml (18–20oz) of breast milk or formula a day, inclusive of milk used in sauces, puddings and cereals.
- By nine months his day's menu may look something like the following:

Breakfast	Breast feed or 180ml (6oz) of formula milk from a cup
	Oat cereal with milk and fruit *or*
	Wholewheat cereal with milk and fruit *or*
	Baby muesli with milk and fruit
	Toast and butter or fruit spread

Lunch	Braised liver, chopped cabbage and carrots *or*
	Chicken with peach and pasta salad *or*
	Lamb hotpot *or*
	Tuna and egg yolk salad *or*
	Chicken, broccoli and pasta in a cream sauce *or*
	Fish cakes with Brussels sprouts and lyonnaise potatoes
	Fruit and yoghurt
	Drink of well-diluted juice from a cup
Tea	Baked potato with grated cheese and apple *or*
	Cheese and vegetable pizza *or*
	Vegetable lasagne *or*
	Carrot and lentil soup *plus*
	Selection of finger sandwiches or rusks with a savoury spread
	Milk pudding or yoghurt
	Small drink of water from a cup
Bedtime	Breast feed or 180–240ml (6–8oz) of formula milk

Feeding plan
at nine to twelve months

	Week 1	Week 2	Week 3	Week 4
Introduce	Oily fish	Egg white	Dates	Beetroot
	Berries	Grapes	Aubergine	Cucumber
	Pineapple	Artichoke	Currants	Beef

- Your baby should be enjoying three well-balanced meals a day and be able to join in most of the family meals.
- During the final stage of weaning the foods listed above should be introduced as and when you think your baby is ready. This will depend very much on how many teeth your baby has and how well he can chew.
- Each day your baby should have three to four servings of carbohydrates, made up of cereal, wholemeal bread, pasta or potatoes.

- He should also have three to four portions of fruit and vegetables, including raw vegetables, and by the end of one year he should be used to raw salad vegetables.
- At this stage he should be eating lots of finger foods and nearly all his fruit and vegetables should be chopped or sliced, instead of mashed.
- He will also need one portion of animal protein or two of vegetable protein.
- By the end of one year most meat, poultry and fish should be chopped up into small pieces instead of being minced or mashed.
- Different foods should not be all mixed together now. He will be much more aware of colour and texture, so try to make his meals look interesting and appealing.
- Some babies will cut their 2.30pm feed out altogether at this stage. If he is not taking 350ml (12oz) between two feeds and inclusive of the milk used in his food, give him extra cheese and yoghurt.
- By one year he still needs a minimum of 350ml (12oz) a day of breast or formula milk, inclusive of milk used in cereal, sauces and puddings.
- Bottle-fed babies should be encouraged to take all of their breakfast milk from a cup. By the age of one year you should also aim to replace the last bottle of formula with a drink from a cup.
- Cow's milk can be introduced as a drink from the age of one year; it should be full fat, pasteurized, and preferably organic.
- By one year his day's menu may look something like the following:

Breakfast	Breast feed or a drink of formula milk from a cup
	Wholewheat or oat cereal with milk and fruit *or*
	Baby muesli with milk and fruit *or*
	Scrambled egg on toast
	Toast with spread *plus*
	Yoghurt and chopped fruit

Lunch   Cold, creamed chicken with apple and celery salad *or*
                 Beef meat-balls in tomato sauce with cabbage and
                 creamed potatoes *or*
                 Tuna-burgers and mixed vegetables *or*
                 Irish stew with parsley dumplings
                 Drink of water or well-diluted juice from a cup
                 Yoghurt and fresh fruit

Mid-afternoon Drink of milk, water or well-diluted juice from a cup

Tea   Thick soup and savoury sandwiches *or*
                 Vegetarian pizza with green salad *or*
                 Chickpea and spinach croquettes with a home-made
                 tomato sauce *or*
                 Lentil and vegetable lasagne
                 Small drink of milk, water or well-diluted juice from a
                 cup

Bedtime   Breast feed or 180ml (6oz) of formula milk from a cup

Useful addresses and further reading

Black-out lining & roller blinds
Available from all John Lewis Partnership stores throughout the UK.

Breast pumps
Ameda Egnell Ltd
Unit 2, Belvedere Trading Estate
Taunton
Somerset TA1 1BH
Tel: 01823 336362
Fax: 01823 336364

Cotton sleeping bags
Kiddycare (Mail order)
Tel: 01343 890389
Fax: 01309 674646

Baby equipment
The Great Little Trading Company
124 Walcot Street
Bath BA1 5BG
Tel: 0990 673009
Fax: 0990 673010

Express Yourself Bras
www.expressyourselfbras.co.uk

Organizations

Foundation for the Study of Infant Deaths
Artillery House
11–19 Artillery Row
London SW1P 1RT
Tel: 020 7222 8001

Twins and Multiple Births Association (TAMBA)
PO Box 30, Little Sutton
South Wirral L66 1TH
Tel: 08707 703305

Further Reading

The Great Ormond Street New Baby and Child Care Book
(Vermilion 1996)
The Baby and Toddler Sleep Programme by Professor John
Pearce (Vermilion 1997)
Your Child's Symptoms Explained by Dr David Haslam
(Vermilion 1997)
Solve Your Child's Sleep Problems by Dr Richard Ferber
(Dorling Kindersley 1985)
From Contented Baby to Confident Child by Gina Ford
(Vermilion 2000)
The Contented Little Baby Book of Weaning by Gina Ford
(Vermilion 2002)
The Complete Sleep Guide for Contented Babies and Toddler
by Gina Ford (Vermilion 2003)
Potty Training in One Week (Vermilion 2003)
The Contented Child's Food Bible by Gina Ford (Vermilion
2004)

Index